Recruiting and Retaining People

Florence Stone

- Fast track route to hiring the best and locking in top talent

- Covers the key areas of recruitment and retention, from new techniques for expanding your search and finding candidates for hard-to-fill jobs to making the best hiring decision and retaining your high-performance talent pool

- Examples and lessons from some of the world's most successful talent managers, including Cigna, Fujitsu Limited, the U.S. Armed Services, General Electric, Hewlett Packard, Steelcase and AlliedSignal, and ideas from the smartest thinkers, including Frederick Herzberg, Abraham Maslow, Richard Boyatzis, Martha R. A. Fields and Peter D. Weddle

- Includes a glossary of key concepts and a comprehensive resources guide.

PEOPLE

09.04

essential management thinking at your fingertips

First published 2002 by
Capstone Publishing (a Wiley company)
8 Newtec Place
Magdalen Road
Oxford OX4 1RE
United Kingdom
http://www.capstoneideas.com

CIP catalogue records for this book are available from the British Library and the US Library of Congress

ISBN 1-84112-206-8

This book is printed on acid-free paper

Substantial discounts on bulk quantities of Capstone books are available to corporations, professional associations and other organizations. Please contact Capstone for more details on +44 (0)1865 798 623 or (fax) +44 (0)1865 240 941 or (e-mail) info@wiley-capstone.co.uk

Contents

Introduction to ExpressExec

ExpressExec is 3 million words of the latest management thinking compiled into 10 modules. Each module contains 10 individual titles forming a comprehensive resource of current business practice written by leading practitioners in their field. From brand management to balanced scorecard, ExpressExec enables you to grasp the key concepts behind each subject and implement the theory immediately. Each of the 100 titles is available in print and electronic formats.

Through the ExpressExec.com Website you will discover that you can access the complete resource in a number of ways:

» printed books or e-books;
» e-content – PDF or XML (for licensed syndication) adding value to an intranet or Internet site;
» a corporate e-learning/knowledge management solution providing a cost-effective platform for developing skills and sharing knowledge within an organization;
» bespoke delivery – tailored solutions to solve your need.

Why not visit www.expressexec.com and register for free key management briefings, a monthly newsletter and interactive skills checklists. Share your ideas about ExpressExec and your thoughts about business today.

Please contact elound@wiley-capstone.co.uk for more information.

Introduction

In good times and bad, organizations have learned about the impact on achievement of mission and corporate goals of shortage of skilled workers. This chapter identifies the costs of the skill war and importance of retention strategies. Read about:

» the long-term cost of thinking employees dispensable;
» the growing skill gap in the global marketplace that led to the shift from a buyer's to a seller's labor market, even during an economic downturn; and
» discover why a strategic approach to retention has proven more successful than one built solely around more dollars or other single initiatives.

In the late 1980s and early 1990s, as companies lopped off managers in the thousands for reasons of economic survival or reorganization, it made sense for Scott Adams' comic strip character Dilbert to poke fun at the homily, "Employees are our most valuable asset." Dilbert referred to it as "the first great lie of management."

Martha R.A. Fields, an HR authority, in her book *Indispensable Employees*, calls this time "The age of disposable employees." By cutting their fat, organizations became leaner and tougher, better able to compete in the global marketplace. But as the new millennium approached, the stronger organizations found themselves with a problem: a shift from a buyer's to a seller's labor market. Companies found themselves scrambling not just to hire good people, but to keep them, as competitors courted their staff.

There was a significant skill gap – that is, a difference between the technical proficiency necessary in these tougher organizations and the labor force's actual know-how and skills. And it was a trend that was expected to continue – economic growth was expected to remain ahead of population growth through the year 2008. Those employees with the right technological and/or managerial knowledge began to flex their workforce muscle, willing to listen to companies with job offers with bigger or better carrots. The earlier waves of downsizing, reorganization, and change that did away with the traditional "employee contract," which offered good employees a reasonable expectation of long-term employment, had also done away with expected loyalty and commitment from employees.

It didn't hurt, either, if a company could offer better working conditions – with reasonable work hours, staff support, and opportunity for professional growth and internal advancement. Employees saw nothing wrong with taking on a new job, then leaving a few days later for a better job depending on the offer. Companies offered recruitment and retention bonuses, employees asked for raises only a few months after joining a company, and headhunters sought out employees before they had settled behind their new desks.

In the US, a study in 2000 by the Bureau of Statistics found that each month, more than 13% of workers quit to take other positions, or one in seven workers compared to one in ten in 1995. In the same survey, they found 55% of US employees thought often of quitting or planned to quit within a year of employment. After considering their options, almost 50% of professional workers chose self-employment – to solo as temps, freelancers, independent contractors, and so forth.

Ironically, the problem that companies encountered in hanging on to their most valuable talent occurred at around the same time studies were being done to determine the reasons behind corporate success. One major study, first carried out by McKinsey & Company in 1997, entitled "The war for talent," discovered that while certain skills were more important than others, the ability to acquire, develop, and retain key personnel was, indeed, "a driver of corporate performance, one that could serve a business as a competitive advantage for the present and into the future."

A strategic approach to the recruitment/retention problem is needed – one that digs into the roots of high turnover and identifies cultural changes as well as pay and benefit packages that will satisfy employees – rather than the "replacement mentality" HR managers seem prone to. Paying recruitment firms time and time again at higher and higher rates is equivalent to, as Dr John Sullivan, chief talent officer of Agilent Technologies reportedly said, a doctor deciding to increase the speed of transfusion as a patient begins to bleed faster.

Yes, the economy has declined since "The age of indispensable workers" began, to use Fields' term for the seller's labor market, but the battle for talented workers is expected to continue. Talent will remain as a critical element in corporate value chains, enabling companies that win the talent wars to be winners as well in the wars for customers, market share, and profitability in the years to come. This book will point to new sources of employees and factors that can improve employee retention and, most important, the ways in which both can be incorporated into corporate people strategies.

Definition of Terms

The war for talent continues even during the current recession. But boom times have taught companies some new tricks to acquire top employees and techniques to identify the source of high attrition. This chapter goes over the new basics.

» Discover the new techniques companies are using to identify suitable candidates.
» Since recruitment is now a global issue, find out how companies are conducting interviews long distance.
» Since a good job/candidate match is one secret to retention, companies are not limiting selection to the interview alone.
» The exit interview can provide lots of information about why employees leave, provided companies know how to really use it well.

Recruitment and retention have changed dramatically over the last 10 years – and the lexicon associated with them has changed as well. Recruitment still is the identification, interview, and selection of the most qualified job candidate, but new means for achieving this have developed – from online recruitment, which involves the use of Websites to identify both vacancies and individuals seeking new jobs, to simulations in which prospective candidates *demonstrate* their capability rather than simply talk about their qualifications, and videoconferencing, which permits long-distance interviews of prospective hires via videoconferencing technology. Retention of employees has also created a new vocabulary – including the term "employer of choice," or that organization that offers culture, programs, and processes that make it a company that employees are least likely to quit.

If you are to fully understand the subject of recruitment and retention in the new millennium, you need a clear understanding of the terms to be used as you delve into the topic.

So let's get clear on the key terms.

THE WAR FOR TALENT

To begin with, what is the "war for talent?"

The economic boom of the mid- to late-1990s created the phrase "war for talent," coined by McKinsey & Company in 1997. It refers to the competition among organizations for high performers, a competition that continues today, despite the slowdown of the economy. Companies experienced high turnover, or attrition, as employees – even new hires – moved from one job to another for the most challenging and financially rewarding work available to them.

Workers were not always so eager to switch jobs. Layoffs over the previous two decades – whether due to an economic downturn or restructuring of the organization – suggested that employees were "disposable;" that is, human assets weren't critical. Replacement workers could easily be hired because the job market was plentiful. Managements argued that they weren't responsible for employees' job security; rather, employee development – both training and career advancement – was the responsibility of employees. Employees learned quickly. They couldn't depend on their employer for job security, and consequently any feelings of loyalty toward employers dissipated.

EMPLOYEE LOYALTY

What do we mean by "employee loyalty?"

We're talking about employee commitment tied to an organization, one made from the first day of employment in return for guaranteed employment, with a career ladder for promotion, for those employees who show up on time and give more than a full day's work for a full day's pay. During the economic boom, the impact of the past economic downturn, with downsizing after downsizing, likely contributed to the job-hopping that companies experienced among their most talented employees. Past experience had given employees little reason to stay with one employer if a prospective employer had a better offer.

HR managers found themselves occupied with filling one vacancy after another. It was hard to keep employees because many chose to "go solo;" that is, become independent and work on a contractual or freelance basis. Called "contingent workers," these individuals were used to fill workforce gaps. During boom years, many IT experts chose to become consultants and work on contract. During our economic downturn, contingent workers can save employers money, working only during peak job periods or otherwise doing short-term assignments. In the beginning, one thought only about contingent work in relationship to clerical tasks. Temp agencies provided administrative assistance when an assistant was out sick, on maternity leave, or on vacation. But today, contingent work is that and much more. Assignments vary. Attorneys, business executives, HR professionals, software engineers, accountants, hotel workers, nurses and other medical professionals, and technical support staff – all can be contingent workers.

The boom period also prompted companies to study their existing personnel to determine if they could take on more responsibility. It was felt an effective way to fill a vacancy, particularly since experienced workers would bring some loyalty to the company, along with past experience in the company, with them to the job. This led to creation of employee skills inventories. What are those?

EMPLOYEE SKILLS INVENTORIES

An employee skills inventory is exactly what it sounds like: a portfolio of the human resources represented by the staff in a company – a catalog of the individual skills, abilities, and knowledge the company currently has. The concept is far from new. Most organizations have traditionally had personnel files or job histories on each of their employees. The difference lies in how the information is organized. Conventional job histories tend to focus on results accomplished. An employee skills inventory focuses on the skills and attributes that led to those accomplishments.

This is a tool not solely for the multinational firms. Even a relatively small firm – with 100 employees or fewer – could find the time and effort worthwhile. The chief benefit is that, rather than sort through reams of personnel files to identify logical internal candidates for a position, one simply has to search the database of the employee skills inventory. Within a few minutes at most, one would have a list of all employees in the company who come closest to the requirements of a specific vacancy.

Of course, the secret to a user-friendly employee skills inventory is how it is organized. Which means sitting down with IT personnel and determining a limited number of fields – all work-related – for the database. In other words, each field that you create for the database should have strategic or administrative importance. As a start, think in terms of skills/knowledge areas – that is, business-related functions or activities in which the employee has either special knowledge or a proven track record – and career aspirations – that is, either other jobs in the company employees might like to pursue or other parts of the world in which they would like to work. Given the global work environment, you might also want to include a field that identifies second language skills.

RECRUITMENT TECHNIQUES

When HR professionals recruited, they recruited not only offline – through recruitment agencies and headhunters, recruiters for more senior positions, and advertisements in trade magazines and newspapers – but online, on "career sites," or sites on the Internet designed specifically to bring together employers and candidates. But the demand for job candidates prompted companies to consider other techniques, like "job fairs," or events in which various companies promote their recruitment needs. "Job fairs" are often held on college campuses to enable companies to recruit motivated entry-level employees, but they also are held in conjunction with trade associations to help members with their job search.

REFERRALS

Referrals also were tried during the boom years, with tremendous success. What are "referrals?" That is when a current employee refers a friend or neighbor, or another they know, to the company as a prospective employee. Since referrals are found to generate high-performers, employees are even given "bounties," or bonuses, for referrals if the new hires stay for a set period. Since employees feel their reputation is on the line if they refer someone unfit to handle the work, they will only recommend those they would expect to work out well for their employer.

JOB ANALYSIS

Recruitment itself underwent a change. In the past, advertisements began with a process called "job analysis" in which the key requirements of the job are identified. These, then, are written up on a job description, a document that lists the requirements and duties of the position to be filled. The list of requirements and duties included the experience, skills, and education needed.

The job description is completed by the supervisor and person holding a position similar to the one for which the document is being completed. Many managers assume that the same description can be used to fill the current opening as was used for recruitment of the previous job occupant. Not so. At least, the description needs to be reviewed to determine if the job has changed since the position was last open. Responsibilities may differ. The past occupant may have brought skills or developed skills since taking the position that now are critical, given changing times and needs. These need to be reflected in the job description.

During the recruitment process, the job description, then, is used to screen résumés. Prior to interviews, the résumés of all applicants are examined in light of the job description to identify questions for discussion with the candidate.

COMPETENCIES

Increasingly, companies are adapting their approach to preparation of the job analysis, which is an analysis of the tasks that the job demands, to an analysis of the job via competencies. What are "competencies?" They are the skills, abilities, knowledge, and attitudes critical to completing the job. They are identified by interviews with both top performers and mediocre performers in which critical parts of the job are discussed. From those interviews, the interviewer is able to identify those "competencies" critical to superperformers in the job.

The idea for competencies was developed by Richard Boyatzis.

Boyatzis believed that more was needed to select, develop, and reward the right people than a match between job background (educational and job history) and job tasks. So in 1982, Boyatzis conducted a survey of 2000 managers who held 41 different jobs in 12 different public and private organizations. The result was a generic model of managerial competencies applicable in different contexts and organization types. The results of his research were published in his book *The Competent Manager: A Model for Effective Performance*.

In his book, Boyatzis suggested that we too often select a manager from a model in our minds of what a "good manager" should be. We're not aware that personal biases are influencing our judgment. Our idea or mindset may be tied to our own characteristics or to previous successful recruits, or it may even just be "the way it is" in the firm. But whatever the reason, the model has little to do with the strengths demanded by the specific managerial position.

Boyatzis detailed each competency, identifying a number of behaviors that would determine its presence or absence. He specified three levels of a competency and suggested that they would "affect different aspects of the individual's application of a particular competency in a job." The three levels were: motivation; self-image or social role; and skill. For each competency he identified, he had one of these components. So someone who had a high efficiency orientation would be motivated primarily by a high need for achievement, would have a self-image of "I can do better," might see himself or herself as an "innovator," and might exhibit observable skills such as goal-setting, planning and organizing resources efficiently. If the individual had a high concern for influence, he or she might be motivated by a need for power, have a self-image which said "I am very important," might associate social role with status, and might exhibit strong influencing behavior.

Boyatzis intended that his work enable organizations not only to understand why someone behaved as they did, but also how they might behave in specific circumstances – in other words, how they might perform in specific jobs.

As mentioned, Boyatzis' work was designed to improve recruitment and job performance. As such, its focus was on identifying the characteristics of top performers. In the UK, the focus is very different – which may also explain the difference in terminology. In the UK, the word is "competence," not "competency," and the focus is on job standardization. The National Council for Vocational Qualifications focuses on defining the tasks and outcomes required of the job, then using this information to set standards or expected outcomes.

INTERVIEWS

Interviews or means of screening prospective hires one-on-one have also changed. As HR managers and supervisors discovered that a major cause for attrition was mismatch between the wants of a prospective hire and the demands of a job, companies moved into "panel interviews;" that is, rather than a single individual interviewing job candidates, each candidate would be interviewed by a group from the company – sometimes members of the work team in which the recruit would work, sometimes members of management from throughout the organization.

Where hires weren't located in the same city – maybe, even the same country – technologically savvy managers and HR professionals began to use videoconferencing to reduce the cost of interviewing hires not easily accessible for a traditional interview.

We may see more of this videoconferencing. Companies around the world have imposed restrictions on travel – national and international – because of the events of September 11, 2001. Rather than pay for a likely hire to visit headquarters for an interview, videoconferencing may be an easier way to begin discussions.

There is a downside to the use of videoconferencing – actually there are two issues to consider. First, you need to ensure good transmission quality. The technology is very much better, but problems can arise that can lead to choppy video and sound glitches. So you want to have the best technicians on hand – both where you are and where the candidate is. Second, participants have to be given an opportunity to feel comfortable with the technology. Those who have yet to see themselves on a television screen may feel uneasy at first. But after the first four or five minutes, most participants forget about the equipment because they are absorbed by what is being discussed.

SIMULATIONS

Besides discussion, companies have begun to verify the statements of candidates – again, to ensure a good job match. So companies have started to use "simulations." What are "simulations?"

They are "try-outs" in which prospective hires are asked to perform one or more tasks that are part of the job. We know that an administrative assistant wouldn't be hired without testing her computer skills. Now, increasingly, companies are applying that same logic when hiring managers, with job simulations designed to simulate the environment, tasks, and challenges the candidate would face if he or she got the job. A simulation, for instance, might require the applicant to respond to e-mail and voicemail messages, meet with a direct report, work closely with colleagues to solve a problem, and present his or her strategic plans during a meeting with the boss.

HR managers or trained assessors play the roles of direct report, co-workers, and/or boss. They evaluate the candidate's performance on everything from strategic thinking and decision-making to collaboration and coaching. Each skill is evaluated in comparison to established job requirements.

The process itself may take anywhere from a half day to two days, which may seem like a big time, but it depends on the position under consideration. Where there is clearly a big benefit to good fit the first time out, then it is clearly worthwhile. In addition, participants completing the assessment process get feedback about their abilities that may be helpful whether or not they get the job.

Simulations aren't always useful in the hiring process when an internal candidate is applying for a job very similar to his or her current position, if training is planned no matter who is hired, or if the difference between a poor performer and an outstanding performer will have little impact on the firm. Simulations make sense if the position is pivotal to the organization's success, the cost of a bad hiring decision is high (from low morale to lost customers and missed sales), when the new hire needs to hit the ground running, or there is a significant difference between the candidate's current position and the prospective position.

PERSONNEL DATABASES

To identify likely candidates for interview and consideration, companies have begun to develop personnel databases with résumés acquired over time - via past ads, mail and Web queries about prospective jobs, and referrals. Companies that use online recruitment "screen" or review incoming résumés using their database, which is designed to pick up key phrases. Such a system is needed given the hundreds upon hundreds of responses an online ad can generate.

Once the decision is made about which candidate to hire, the process is not over. Managers know about the importance of "orientation," that is, helping the employee to adapt to the new job from his or her first day. In many companies, before new employees actually start their jobs, the HR department will provide a briefing about the company. They may be shown videos, be given a tour of the facilities, receive literature, or attend a lecture. They learn the history of the organization, the benefits they will receive, and the rules and regulations by which they will have to operate.

ORIENTATION

But managers and supervisors have learned about the need to augment this with an orientation of the team or department. The quality of the orientation program has been found to have an impact not only on future performance of new hires, but on job satisfaction and retention.

Some managers choose to give a new hire a "buddy" or team pal to work with him or her and familiarize the new recruit to the workplace. Others spend time, devoting a little extra effort coaching the employee; that is, tutoring the new hire in his or her job until the person has mastered the new job.

RETENTION

Studies show that employees leave for many reasons, and a poor relationship with their supervisor is a major one. Early coaching goes far to demonstrate to an employee that his or her supervisor wants him or her to succeed. In his book *Love 'Em or Lose 'Em: Getting Good People to Stay* (Bettett-Koehler, 1999), author S. Jordan-Evans observed, "People don't quit companies, they quit bosses." Evidence has shown a high correlation between employee job satisfaction and the relationship between the employee and direct supervisors and managers.

In terms of retention strategies, any efforts to reduce turnover should be preceded by study of contents of exit or separation interviews. Exit or separation interviews are meetings, usually one-on-one with HR professionals, to probe the reason why a person is choosing to leave a job and to get from the employee information about the job or the company that may cause discontent.

Companies have found that exit interviews tend to have little payoff. Most employees are reluctant to burn their bridges and consequently to share their true feelings about their job, their supervisor, or the company, and consequently they are more likely to talk about the new job to which they are going than the work conditions of their current job. This has led to post-separation interviews; that is, interviews held six to eight months after an employee has quit to elicit much more meaningful information.

HERZBERG AND MASLOW

However companies determine their insights, most have found some commonalities. To understand them, we have to go back to the work of two well-known motivational researchers: Frederick Herzberg and Abraham Maslow.

Herzberg's work on job satisfaction may seem unrelated to recruitment and retention, but it is very much so. If you think about the years of economic prosperity, it was very much a buyer's market, with the decision where to work pretty much dependent on the desires and needs of employees and managers. Likewise, the issue of retention. If a job wasn't what an individual wanted, he or she could look elsewhere and be assured of finding another one within a few weeks or a month or two, at most. The economy has changed, and many employees are out of work. The equation has shifted in favor of management, but only so far – it may take longer to find another job, but your most talented employees should still be able to leave. And given the lean, post-downsized organizations, their loss may be significantly felt.

Herzberg's work identified those factors that make the difference between job satisfaction and dissatisfaction. He called those factors that influence satisfaction "hygiene factors." They include a good relationship with manager or supervisor, interpersonal relationships, physical working conditions, salary, company policies and administrative practices, benefits, and job security. Herzberg wrote: "When these factors deteriorate to a level below that which the employee considers acceptable, then job dissatisfaction ensures." Interestingly, it is not their existence but their lack of existence that has an impact on motivation – and, I would contend, on contentment with a work environment.

Herzberg's book *The Motivation to Work* (1959) focused on hygiene factors. But a later article, entitled "One more time: how do you motivate employees" (*Harvard Business Review*, 1968), suggests more specific actions that companies can take to retain employees in good and bad times. In the article, Herzberg coined the term "job enrichment," which suggested how organizations could generate employee enthusiasm by providing more opportunity for them to use their creativity. If you look at "employers of choice," you see evidence of job enrichment – career management, self-development, self-managed learning, even empowerment. Gary Hamel said, "Pay for performance, employee stock ownership plans, end-of-year bonuses – too many organizations seem to believe that the only motivation to work is an economic one. Teaching knowledge assets like Skinnerian rats is hardly the way to get the best out of people. Herzberg offered a substantially more subtle approach – one that still has much to recommend it."

Maslow is best known for his "hierarchy of needs" – a concept he first published in 1943. Maslow argued that there was an ascending order of needs that need to be understood for people to be motivated. First, there are the physiological needs of warmth, shelter, and food. Once these basic needs are met, others emerge to dominate. Next comes the safety needs, then social or love needs, and then ego or self-esteem needs. Ultimately, with each need satisfied comes what Maslow labeled "self-actualization," the individual achieves his or her own personal potential.

Maslow's work had a significant impact on his time, moving management to implement participative management programs in the early 1960s to satisfy higher needs. During the economic boom, organizations had in place motivational/retention strategies that were designed to make employees feel self-actualized. After all, all lower needs were satisfied. And, as Maslow's research indicated, such lower needs must be satisfied before higher needs are addressed.

As downsizings increase, we may see lower needs of concern – in particular, issues of job security. We can expect issues of loyalty as employees question whether they should remain with a company in which their most basic need – for money to feed and house themselves and family – is not guaranteed. This can lead to continued turnover despite a tight job market.

03

Evolution

The war for talent began in the 1980s with the birth of the Information Age? Not so. To find out when it truly began, read this chapter, which looks at:

» the 20% decline in birth rate in the 1950s and 1960s;
» the impact of poor educational systems on graduates of the 1970s and early 1980s combined with rapidly changing technology; and
» the age of dispensable employees with wave of downsizing after downsizing and its impact on employee loyalty.

One of the major challenges facing employers as we go from the twentieth into the twenty-first century – and we make the complete transition from the Industrial Age to the Information Age – is finding and keeping good employees. To fully understand the situation facing organizations worldwide, we need to discuss:

» the drop in the birth rate in the late 1950s and early 1960s that has caused a significant drop in the numbers of people in the employment pool. And, more important, the insufficient supply today of ''good'' workers in practically every field;
» the decade of the 1980s and its impact on the traditional employment contract that guaranteed employees work provided they did a good job and employee attitudes toward their employers in return;
» the loss of loyalty, on both sides;
» the economic upturn in the late 1990s that demanded high performers yet found the most wanted employees in a position to call their own tune;
» the technological revolution that led to numerous dotcom startups with their demand for technological talent; and
» the dotcom shakeout that released talented techies, but also competition from among brick and click operations for these individuals.

Some people would say that the war for talent began in the 1980s with the birth of the Information Age – as hard assets like machines, factories, and capital were seen as less important than intangibles like brand loyalty, intellectual capital, and job experience and know-how. During the heart of the Industrial Age, only 17% of all jobs required knowledge workers; now almost 60% require knowledge workers. Or, more important, ''talented'' workers. As John Chambers, CEO of Cisco Systems said, ''I'd rather hire a single world-class engineer and five of his or her peers than 200 run-of-the-mill engineers.''

THE LATE 1950S AND EARLY 1960S

But to really understand the recruitment/retention situation facing industrialized countries, you have to go further back than the 1980s to the late 1950s and early 1960s, which experienced a drop in the birth rate. In the US alone, the decline of 20% below the accustomed rate has produced a shortfall of 5 million Americans in the workforce and is expected to increase to 7 million by 2008 since the birth rate, while it increased after the "baby bust" years, never did return to the previous level.

The gap between jobs and those to fill it would be greater, but we can expect to see many baby boomers remain in the workforce either because they enjoy working or would lack the funds otherwise.

JOHNNY CAN'T READ

Fast forward, and we see large numbers of youngsters of the 1950s and 1960s graduating from high school yet unable to read, write, or think. Some college graduates weren't of much higher caliber. The problem was complicated by the rapidly changing technology. But the situation wasn't seen as grave, although increasingly during the late 1960s and 1970s you could find articles extolling businesses to get involved in the problems of education to ensure Johnny could read.

Skill deficiencies weren't so severe that companies could not find the people they wanted. The early 1980s were prosperous times. The baby boomers had blossomed into mature adults and were spending future earnings with something called credit cards. The job market was robust. From the perspective of various businesses, employees could leave if they wished; there was always someone waiting who would gladly take their job.

Then came what one author – Martha R. A. Fields of *Indispensable Employees* – has called "The age of dispensable employees." It was the late 1980s and early 1990s, and western organizations found themselves under significant pressure for consumer dollars by foreign firms, particularly those in Japan. In the US, for one, sales and the economy plummeted. Companies in the industrialized nations looked at their businesses, and they recognized a need to run tighter ships, in some instances to reorganize, in other instances redirect efforts.

THE AGE OF DISPENSABLE EMPLOYEES

This led to the wave upon wave of downsizing, reorganization, and change. In turn, this caused widespread employee anxiety, insecurity, and cynicism. If there were a marker that could be placed on the front stoops of the leaner corporations that resulted, the downsized employees might have it say: "Dead: Company loyalty."

Until then, employees believed there was a social contract between them and their employer, one in which those employees who showed up on time and gave more than a full day's work for a full day's pay were secure. If you could, you stayed in the same company. It made sense for an employee to devote 30 to 40 years to an organization if the company had career tracks that ensured advancement for those who put in that 110%. With downsizing, the belief died, along with any sense of commitment on the part of employees. Yes, in the past, there had been layoffs, but these downsizings had been followed by periods of rehirings. As companies across full industries cut back staff, people who were let go by one employer no longer could go to another company in the same industry and find work at the same level for the same or more money.

Employees who had jobs stayed where they were regardless of the working conditions. Survivors of the corporate ax, they tolerated the lean organizations with their long working hours and limited, if any, advancement opportunities.

Actually companies had it good as far as recruitment went until the economy perked up. The talent was available for the picking. But as the economy improved, companies found themselves in need of employees who could help them move agendas further, boost sales, and further build the company. From a buyer's market, companies now had moved into a seller's market as skilled and talented employees began to recognize their value and worth. Working for the same firm – showing loyalty to one employer over one or two decades – wasn't worth it; after all, the mid 1980s and early 1990s had shown that employers weren't loyal to them. If they left their current employer, they could find another that was willing to pay a substantial increase in salary as well as offer such carrots as stock options, trips to exotic locations, and a sign-on bonus.

If you look at the résumés of individuals during that period, you discover four or five jobs over a five-year period. The younger employees who had seen their parents work hard yet be unable to keep their jobs entered the workforce with an "I'm in it for myself" mentality that was viable given the competitive job market. Those who stayed in the same job over time found they could demand a retention bonus plus a pay/benefits package equivalent to that from a job switch. Turnover was high. After all, with online recruitment available to employees, it was easier to find a new job. And the old taboos against job-hopping had evaporated. Indeed, if you were with the same company for more than five years, the recruiter questioned your worth.

Ironically, Peter Drucker had predicted in 1980 just this situation in his book *Managing in Turbulent Times*. Increasingly, he proposed, workers would see their employers as little more than temporary work environments. Loyalty and allegiance would be to one's discipline or professional, not to a specific business. So length of service at any one company would be shorter than in the past. He had foreseen the impact of low birth rates on the labor force and that those entering the workforce would have high expectations, too often at variance with what managements were offering. Most important, he projected the increase in numbers of "knowledge workers." Drucker's genius notwithstanding, evidence of these developments were already present, yet these signs went unnoticed by employers.

COMPETITIVE ADVANTAGE

A study by McKinsey & Company entitled "The war for talent", first published in 1997 and updated in 2000, found that 99% of the corporate officers surveyed felt their management pools needed to be stronger three years from then. Only 20% said they had enough talented leaders to pursue most of their company's goals. It was this study that brought to the business press's attention the seriousness of the shortage of talent worldwide. In tracing the source of the word "talent" itself, McKinsey made clear how critical people were to a company's bottom line. The survey's findings demonstrated an awareness by leadership of the companies surveyed that performance and competitiveness could only be achieved via better talent – in other words, talent was the means to competitive advantage.

According to the McKinsey study and the subsequent book *The War for Talent* by Ed Michaels, Helen Handfield-Jones, and Beth Axelrod, all with McKinsey, the term referred to a unit of weight. Just as talent is part of a value chain in a company's success, so were talents of precious metals exchanged a measure of monetary value. This monetary meaning is evident in the New Testament's Parable of the Talents in which St Matthew tells the tale of a lord who gave eight talents to his three servants, two of whom worked hard and doubled the value of their talents. The third, who was lazy, buried his talent in the ground, and lost his position as a consequence. Later, in the sixteenth century, Martin Luther interpreted this parable to mean that it was God's will that people exercise their innate talents through hard work, thus forming the basis of the Protestant work ethic. As the term talent has become more abstract in meaning, it has come to reflect the most effective leaders and managers at all levels who can help a company meet its objectives – in the language of strategic planning, a "corporate driver." As Jim Robbins, CEO of Cox Communications, observed, "Talent is the single gating factor for us in realizing our growth vision." Enron board chairman Kenneth Lay said, "The only thing that differentiates Enron from our competition is our talent."

In greatest demand during the talent wars has been those with technology skills. As dotcom after dotcom launched on the Internet in the mid-1990s to 1999, these Internet upstarts drew to them those with the critical know-how. With job responsibilities and pay packages/benefits beyond their experience, not to mention offerings of stock options once the startup went public, candidates quickly hired on. As brick and mortar firms spun off click operations, they, too, offered pay and benefits packages above normal to bring on board the IT talent they needed. More traditional businesses with the need for skilled IT experts, organizations like transport firms and consumer banks, found it tough to get the people they needed. Increasingly, companies in industrialized nations began to seek talent from abroad where, in the beginning, it was available. But as the economic good times expanded around the world, companies in these industrializing countries fought back, looking for ways to make local talent stay put.

Clearly recruitment and retention are not only issues of a single nation. In examining the changing roles of the HR function in a globally competitive marketplace, a study by the Development Dimensions International's (DDI) HR Benchmark Group entitled "The globalization of human resource practices" identified recruitment of high-quality employees as second priority over the coming two years. The study found, as previously mentioned, that job candidates were just not as qualified for specific roles, or multi-tasked posts, as they had been. Those who have the skills are quickly snatched up. But the problem internationally wasn't simply lack of talent, but the ability of qualified applicants to work across political and cultural boundaries.

The same DDI survey identified employee retention as a priority for global HR. It spoke about the "unease" over the number of resignations within the firms surveyed, a fear supported by another DDI retention study that found one-third of all global employees surveyed expected to leave for another job within the next year.

THE OTHER SIDE OF THE COIN

Recruitment was tough. Retention has been tougher. Increasingly employees were leaving full-time jobs to set up their own businesses. In 2000 in the US, contingency workers accounted for almost 50% of the professional workforce. Companies found among their staff individuals labeled "passive applicants," individuals who were not seeking a new job but were not adverse to considering working on their own or hearing out a headhunter or recruiter who had an offer. High-growth firms like Dell Computer, with its need for 100 new employees each month, would seek out employees via the business news about mergers and reorganizations. One trick of some recruiters is to hang about newsgroups to identify talented techies, then follow them to their corporate intranet, and contact them, offering a job interview. Clearly, such inquiries interested the recipients. A study by the US Bureau of Statistics showed that 55% of US employees think often of quitting or plan to quit within a year, thereby supporting the DDI global study's results. The average public company was losing half its employees every four years. Efforts at retention weren't very successful – only 9% in the Bureau of Statistics survey felt comfortable with their results. The costs were considerable. According to Peter Tobia, co-author of the Kepner-Tregoe study "Avoiding the brain drain: What companies are doing to lock in their talent," employers too often failed to see the total costs of turnover. "The loss of high performers costs more than money. It tends to impair the organization's memory, dilutes the ability to perform, and compromises the will to win. In short," he concluded, "it saps the organization of its vitality."

In dollars alone, it cost companies from $10,000 to $50,000 to replace and retrain a lost employee. Consider that in terms of turnover – 50% of a company's employees every four years – and the costs of replacement as they might appear on the bottom of an operating statement become evident as well.

As the economy has cooled off, the question being asked is, "Will the recruitment/retention frenzy continue?" With the demise of numerous dotcoms in 1999 and early 2000, there was available IT talent. But many of those have been scooped up. Brick and click operations continue to be birthed as legacy firms see the value of a Web presence. The dotcom shakeout may have shifted individuals' views about their careers – away from the risky Internet and toward IT/Internet roles in legacy firms – but we can expect a continuation of Internet startups, with more realistic business models we can only hope, and other small businesses that will absorb available talent.

LOOKING TO THE FUTURE

Based on birth rates in the 1960s and 1970s, we can also antici-pate a dearth in number of 25 to 44 year olds – the demographic segment that supplies organizations' leadership for the most part. The posts that could go unfilled may require older executives to postpone retirement, although the average of age of retirement has remained constant – between 62 and 63 – for the last 20 years. We can anticipate "The age of indispensables" to last for several decades, a reflection of the growing demand for high-caliber managerial and technological talent. And we will see the issue of employee retention continue to take up HR management's time as employees see the professional and financial benefit from switching from one company to another.

TIMELINE

- 1950s–1960s: Decline in birth rate.
- 1960s–1970s: Johnny can't read. First graduates with deficient reading, writing, thinking skills.
- 1970s–1980s: Prosperous times.

- **Mid-1980s:** Downsizing, reorganizing, change; employee job insecurity.
- **Early 1990s:** Loyalty – employer, employee – dead.
- **Mid-1990s:** Robust economy; dotcom startups; low unemployment and talent war (recruitment/retention problems).
- **1999:** Sluggish economy; threat of recession; dotcom shakeout.
- **2000:** Talent war continues but recruitment at slower pace; retention still a problem.
- **2001:** Projections of continued shortfall in talented managers, technicians for long term.

04

The E-Dimension

Any discussion of recruitment and retention today must include mention of how evolving technology – in particular, the Web – has changed the situation. This chapter examines:

» the growing online recruitment industry;
» the use of the Web to capture "passive job seekers;"
» the role of a well-designed Website on recruitment; and
» the use of a corporate intranet to market corporate benefits to employees and managers and reduce attrition.

Any discussion of recruitment today must include mention of how evolving technology – in particular, the Web – has changed the field. Here we will examine:

» the growing online recruitment industry;
» the impact on labor relations of online recruitment;
» the e-dimension's impact on "passive job seekers;"
» the role of your Website, intentional and unintentional, on recruitment; and
» leveraging online recruitment: how to market your firm electronically.

The Internet has changed the way employers think about finding good employees: not only techies, but talent in all the business disciplines. Think about it: there are some 18 million résumés posted just on Monster.com, the largest Internet job site. Monster.com claims almost half a million jobs available worldwide. There are more than 5000 job boards where résumés and job opportunities are posted.

So the Web has become the most effective way to disseminate information about the availability of jobs and people broadly.

HR STALKERS SEEKING OUT POTENTIAL NEW HIRES

But, surprise, that's only a small way that the new technology has influenced the hiring game. For instance, recruiters can use the Internet to access millions of other résumés and biographical data posted on the Internet not intended for job searches. What? All it takes is a tenacious recruiter interested in recruiting someone with specific skills, like C++ or Java programming skills. The recruiter can visit newsgroups and identify likely candidates, then follow these individuals back to their firms, identify them in staff listings, and finally cold-call them about a job change.

Most corporate intranets are accessible. It doesn't take a hacker to get in to view the employee list. There is no law against visiting, but such sites too often reveal more than an outsider should see.

The result of such a search could be a rich list of skilled employees who could make excellent recruits. Maybe they aren't looking for a new job, but they might be induced to consider a job change with the right offering. These candidates are called "passive applicants" in the recruitment business jargon, and as employee loyalty has eroded, their numbers have grown.

After all, as employees have seen co-workers downsized, rightsized, or otherwise displaced, why should they be concerned about the impact their departure might have on their current employer? In Spring 2001, Wetfeet.com, a recruitment management firm, reported results of a survey that showed that 36% of employees surveyed, though happy with their current jobs, would be willing to move within six months if something better came along. So online recruiting has leveled the playing field between employer and employee, according to Peter Cappelli, a professor of management at the Wharton School of Business.

THE NEW PLAYING FIELD

"Issues of fairness with things like compensation, opportunities, etc. [used to be] all based on internal criteria. Now, increasingly, they are based on external criteria," says Cappelli. Rate of pay, job title, position – all used to be based on seniority. Now, he observes, they are increasingly based on the rate for similar jobs elsewhere. Which makes the employment relationship comparable to a market relationship.

Consequently, the Internet has better positioned employees in the job marketplace. However, it has also made it a lot easier for an employer to hire talent from the outside than it once was. Given access to online recruitment services, not to mention passive recruiting, companies need not think about growing talent within the organization. They can get the skills they need now, without training or development.

Those staff databases that were created five to ten years ago to enter valuable information about the competencies of existing employees have less purpose for promotion from within. On the other hand, as you will discover if you read on, the concept of a database hasn't been lost. But now it is part of the recruitment effort.

Which brings us to the topic of electronic recruitment.

THE GROWTH OF ONLINE RECRUITMENT

No question, online recruiting has grown significantly – and in a very short time. In the beginning, most of the companies that used it were large and they saw it as the best way to reach out to technical personnel, but that has changed. This may be due to the feedback from these corporate giants that electronic recruitment produced the greatest number of applicants as well as some of their best hires, second only to employee referrals. Even organizations that scorned online recruitment now use it, like the US Central Intelligence Agency (CIA). According to Gary Cluff, national staffing director, the CIA has gone from being scornful about online recruitment to using it to make "same-day offers;" about 15% of its new hires come from the Web. At Internet Corporation, a manufacturer of cast metal auto parts, online recruitment accounts for as much as 90% of the people for the firm's Stevensville, Michigan facility; traditional recruitment just hasn't worked.

As companies on fast-track growth paths, online recruitment allows them access to the global workforce. In developing and newly industrialized countries, this has made it hard to keep national talent at home. On the other hand, it has offered visibility to managers and employees that might not have been available in the past.

A study by Forrester Research projects that by 2003 about $1.7bn will be spent in online recruitment, a significant increase from the $105mn spent in 1999. There's reason for this.

A COMPARISON OF OFFLINE AND ONLINE RECRUITMENT

First and foremost, online recruitment continues to be less costly than its print counterpart, averaging 5% of the price of placing a help wanted ad in a major newspaper for 30 days. Cost is based not on the size of the ad, as with print, but either by individual posting or subscription. Costs can range from $100 to $200 per posting on a site to $500 per month for 10 postings plus access to the résumé database, to $100,000 a year for unlimited postings and database access. Some sources offer free trial subscriptions, which enables an organization to assess the site's traffic and decide if it's a good investment.

Think $100,000 seems like a lot? Compare that cost to what your firm would have to pay for a display ad in a metropolitan newspaper. It could be as high as $2000 a day, and that single ad might have to run several weeks until sufficient responses were received to identify enough prospects to begin the interview phase of recruitment.

This raises another advantage of online recruitment.

Online recruitment generates faster responses from prospective employees, thereby shortening the hiring cycle. With well-written résumés and job postings, screening time can also be cut.

WRITING YOUR ONLINE AD

What makes either a well-written résumé or job ad on the Web? The secret to both is the use of "key words" – that is, words based on those factors critical to the job being sought or one advertised or descriptive of the job. After all, jobs aren't listed alphabetically, but rather accessible via a search function.

No doubt, there is a danger that you could unintentionally eliminate some good prospects, but the assumption made is that the best candidates for a position are familiar with the jargon of the field and will use those phrases in their résumés and searches and, likewise, positions posted will reflect the jargon of the field. If you do decide to use a job title, don't simply ask for a "manager." Clarify, like "manager, retail book publishing" or "manager, fast-food outlet."

Margaret Dikel, a recruitment consultant and creator of *The Riley Guide*, an Internet directory, warns against postings that are too broad or too narrow. Too narrow, and applicants won't be able to find it. Too broad, and the posting will generate responses that may not fit the job. In terms of the content of an ad you post for your company, you might want to keep these three rules from Peter D. Weddle, publisher of *Weddle's: The Newsletter For Successful Online Recruiting*, in mind.

» Create intriguing headings; use focus groups of new hires to review postings to ensure that you use suitable phrases for searchability as well as word the ad to interest prospective candidates.
» Summarize the job in the first five lines.
» Identify pay range within the first five lines.

Where should you post your ads? The turbulence of the industry is evident if you compare the 2000 and 2001 *Weddle's Recruiter's Guide to Employment Web Sites*. Twenty-three of the sites in the 2000 Guide no longer exist or have radically changed, whereas the 2001 Guide has 147 new sites. Further, current sites offer new capabilities from just a year ago. For instance, limitations of length of job postings seem to be disappearing. And most general purpose sites offer some form of buyer incentive, with volume and multi-user discounts and job posting-résumé searching packages the most frequent.

Sites fall into two groups: general sites, like People Online and Monster.com, and niche sites, based on career, geography, industry, or association or other affinity group, like CareersColorado, Seek (Australia), ElectricJob.com, ministryjobs.com, HireHealth.com, or Black.Online. In a recent comparison of recruitment sites, Peter Weddle found that traffic to the general sites was significantly higher than to the niche sites, as might be expected, but, also as you might expect, candidates to the niche sites were more likely to fit job specifications. What kinds of numbers are we talking about? Nurses for a Healthier Tomorrow was around 1000 per month whereas ComputerJobs.com got over 473,000 visitors monthly. In terms of general sites, you had a site like People Online, a site in Brazil, with 123 visitors each month to Monster.com with 4,500,000+ visitors each month; the average was around 300,000 visitors per month for the general sites, according to Weddle.

In picking where to post an ad, traffic numbers may be less important than site track records in the fields for which you are seeking new hires, as Weddle observes. Just as traffic isn't so important, neither is database size. Depending on the sites, robust résumé databases can be found at both niche and general sites. Your concern should be that the demographics of the database match the profile of previous successful employees in the posted position. This is more important, even, than the age of résumés; that is, the length of time résumés remain on the database. In today's job market, a résumé no more than 90 days old suggests someone who is actively looking for a job, but résumés two years or older may be a good source for potential candidates as well. Their authors may not be actively seeking jobs anymore, but they may be ready to move on, for in today's job market résumés of two+ years often belong to someone who has been in their present position for over a year and a half and are ready for their next move.

Finally, in making your selection of sites to post ads, according to Weddle, if possible, choose sites that contain software that alerts passive job seekers that a position has been posted that matches the "ideal job" they described when they were at the site. This extends your recruiting arm beyond job-seeking candidates. Certainly these sites have an appeal to job seekers. Curious HR managers have occasionally unintentionally stumbled on résumés posted by staff members, even new recruits, and some companies have imposed tough penalties under such circumstances – even termination. "Job agents," as this software is called, prevent this from happening.

As you use recruitment sites, periodically stop to measure their success. Consider the number of applicants generated, cost-per-applicant, and the quality of the candidates.

CORPORATE WEBSITES

While much attention focuses on the career sites out there in which job openings are posted and résumés can be found, a company's own Website often is as effective as these recruitment sites to secure job candidates' names and résumés. Because recruitment information can be lost on your company's Website, you may want to have a separate recruiting Website created for human resources. If you can't do that, see if you can have designed a special recruiting page and put a link on the home page so applicants can easily access the recruiting page.

Those organizations that have the most success with Web-page recruiting are the well-known corporations. Job seekers turn first to them. That doesn't mean that you have to work for Oracle or Dell, or Yahoo! to attract job candidates via the Internet. Companies that are known and respected in their industries will attract people who have worked in that industry. If you can do so, link sites in the field to your recruitment page.

You can also draw prospective job candidates to the site by including the Web address in offline help-wanted adds. And don't forget advertising the Website in technical and professional journals.

If you can get a page or more on the company Website, use the space effectively. Don't design the page yourself; get a Web-page designer to plan a format that will stand out and make it easy for applicants to locate the jobs in which they may be interested. You can use the site to list specific openings or encourage job hunters to submit their résumés.

Where specific openings are listed, be sure to include answers to these questions:

» What is the nature of the job?
» What skills will the employee use on the job?
» What are the key requirements for being considered for this job?
» What training will the company give the new employee?
» What is the pay range?
» What are some other benefits of working for your firm? Since numbers of visitors will fall into the category of passive job seekers, make submission of an online résumé fast and simple.

Need to stimulate interest in your firm? Use links to help visitors obtain information about the company that will influence their decision to submit a résumé.

Put on your marketing hat. You want to entice them to take the first step to submit a résumé to your firm. To do that, emphasize the opportunities in working for your firm, not the requirements or hard work, or recent need to downsize for economic or strategic reasons.

If you use the recruitment pages to prospect for job candidates, not solely to fill vacancies, you may want to let candidates know more about the company's facilities, culture and value system, and employee development opportunities, as well as recruitment opportunities. Web pages worth study are those maintained by Dell Computer, which includes a "Dell InterviewPak" with maps, directions, lists of restaurants near the Dell facility, current weather forecasts, and local cost of living in comparison to that in bigger cities within the state.

WANTED: OUTSTANDING CAREER SITES

At least one-third of unemployed professional, managerial, and technical employees use electronic means in their job search. Even applicants for nonmanagerial positions will visit the Web during their job search. So companies need to include electronic recruitment in efforts to attract new employees. Failure to use electronic recruitment can leave you with vacant positions long after companies with less attractive recruitment offers have filled theirs. Certainly, a tour of cutting edge companies shows their appreciation of the Web as a recruitment device.

Even today, as some of these companies cut back staff for strategic reasons, these firms continue to recruit off the Web to support new business directions.

If you want to see two well designed recruitment sites, visit Cisco Systems and Dell Computer. While the topsy-turvy economy hasn't left them untouched, their sites continue to reach out to potential hires. After all, you never know when you might find among the candidates a genius with the next technological breakthrough idea.

During the best of times in the late 1990s, Cisco was hiring over 1000 employees each quarter, still a lot less than Dell, which averaged about 100 new hires each week to sustain its growth. Both organizations have the same objective: to hire the best engineering and business talent out there. About one-third of Dell's new hires come from dell.com. Cisco Systems receives 81% of its résumés electronically.

At the Dell site, candidates can check for openings on the site's "job cart" or they can submit their résumé. To help them submit a résumé compatible to Dell's recruitment database, Dell offers a résumé writing tool to facilitate submission. If you aren't sure if Dell is where you want to work, you can download an interview packet courtesy of Dell that includes information not only on benefits, but also life in Austin, TX, where Dell is headquartered, and Lebanon, TN, where the company has manufacturing, technical, support, and sales staff; Dell community activities, including The Dell Foundation, a corporate charitable foundation focused on preparing young people primarily in Texas and Tennessee for the digital economy; online employee giving programs and volunteerism that mobilizes Dell employees to address worldwide needs; its Diversity Difference program that recognizes "that our universe of differences and similarities offer a universe of possibilities and opportunities;" and finally its workforce development program that ensures that Dell employees are the top in their field.

Whereas the Dell site is only in English, Cisco Systems' site has been written in English, Cantonese, Mandarin, and Russian. It tries to be not only informative, but also entertaining. For instance, while Cisco has a tool to help in résumé submissions so that information offered is more readily matched against job openings, tying each subsequent question to the previous answer submitted by a prospective applicant, it also created an "Uh, oh, My Boss Is Coming" button that allows an applicant to turn the form into something more innocent if their manager walks by.

Cisco also recognizes the value that comes from better understanding the culture of a prospective employer. A page entitled MakeFriends@Cisco links individuals interested in working at Cisco with current employees, who will talk to them about life at Cisco and potential job opportunities. Cisco employees volunteer for the program, which matches them with recruits based on the information potential applicants have submitted.

Besides its own site, Cisco also posts job openings on career sites. It tries to target the most qualified talent available, and consequently it runs focus groups of its own staff to identify work practices, interests, and lifestyles of the most successful engineers and managers. The results help make decisions about where to post recruitment ads or place corporate banners. There is a special HotJobs@Cisco page at hotjobs.com, for instance, but you may also come upon a corporate banner at Dilbert Zone.

WEBSITE BASICS

Whether you use the Web pages to advertise openings or identify future hiring prospects, each page of the Website should contain e-mail, fax, telephone number, and street address. Within the HR Department, there should be one individual assigned responsibility to respond to all inquiries in a timely manner as well as read, screen, and respond to all résumés submitted through the site. An up-to-date site is critical to ongoing attention from suitable candidates; experts recommend jobs remain no more than 30 days on a Website before being removed. Post weekly new jobs, and review submissions daily.

If you get lots of résumés, you may want to use an automated system that "reads" résumés for specific criteria and then transfers the information from the résumés into an applicant database organized so you and your co-workers can search the information. The system works very much like an external recruitment Website, scanning résumés for key words and phrases. Applicant tracking systems have been in use for some time but, more recently, more progressive companies have installed hiring management systems that go beyond matching applicants with positions to writing ads and maintaining information on recruitment efforts – from the number of résumés received for a position, to offer made, to the level of performance of the candidate chosen.

BESIDES THE INTERNET...

While we talk about electronic recruiting, we shouldn't forget to touch on interactive voice response to get competency-related information about potential employees. This computer-assisted screening enabled one major clothing manufacturer to save $2.4mn from hiring mistakes during a three-year period – turnover dropped from 87% to 51%. One of the top accounting and consulting firms in the US uses computer-assisted screening online to hire candidates from college. To staff a store in Las Vegas, Nike used computer-assisted screening to make the first cut. Eight questions raised over the phone enabled the firm to move quickly through 3,500 applications for positions in the store. According to Diane Arthur, author of *The Employee Recruitment and Retention Handbook*, the company was looking for candidates with customer service experience, a passion for sports, and values in keeping with Nike's. During a 45-minute video, candidates were asked to choose from among customer service scenarios. Responses were recorded, and areas for further queries were identified.

Those candidates who demonstrated a temperament for service positions then met with interviewers who used competency-based interviewing to make the final cuts.

According to Arthur, Nike attributes computer-assisted screening to its ability to staff up fast and, more important given the cost of turnover, reduce turnover by 21% over two years.

We can expect the use of evolving technology to influence recruitment into the future. There may be some Luddites who still believe the best screening is done by an individual with a stack of paper résumés on their desk followed by a face-to-face interview, and raise concerns about a breach of trust when a résumé is shared without the writer's permission. But the cost and time savings likely will expand computer-based recruitment. Indeed, today, dozens of companies, including Target, Home Depot, and Macy's, are replacing paper applications and in-person interviews not only with online recruiting but also computer kiosks at their stores as an initial screening tool for applicants. They even conduct psychological tests that the companies say match job skills and personalities with the available positions.

The Global Dimension

Unable to find key personnel in their own countries, companies are recruiting from abroad and fighting off efforts by foreign governments to entice foreign nationals back home. This chapter describes:

» the little change in need for global recruiting as the world economy slows;
» how IT personnel continue to head up the list of foreign recruits;
» the technology that has made global recruitment easier;
» the impact that recruitment of locals has had on local markets and how they are fighting back; and
» the effort of developing countries to speed up their technological growth by recruiting from industrialized nations.

We look at how the war for talent is being waged by companies that, unable to find all the key personnel in their own countries, are recruiting from abroad. Here we will discuss the following.

» The little change in need for global recruiting as the world economy slows.
» IT personnel continue to head up the list of foreign recruits but they aren't only individuals being sought.
» The technology that organizations are using to find employees in foreign job markets.
» The impact that recruitment of locals has on local labor markets and how they are fighting back to keep their talent.
» The efforts by developing countries to recruit talent from industrialized nations.

The competition for talent is global. Even as the economy for much of the world shifts from rosy red to somber gray, there continues to be a shortage of skilled workers around the world. The battle is bloodiest in the IT industry – for IT personnel in engineering firms to those for banks, to those for consumer companies, to those for transport businesses – but all disciplines are experiencing some shortfall in number of skilled workers.

THE SHOE IS ON THE OTHER FOOT

For the industrialized nations, during the best of economic times, the search for employees meant looking beyond their borders to developing countries, like India and Thailand. The economy has shifted gears but the search continues, albeit at a slower pace. Indeed, developing nations now worry that they may find themselves without the skilled people they need to grow their countries. Not only in Europe but also in Asia, companies are trying to lure talent back from the US by offering top-of-the-line pay packages. They are even trying to tempt US nationals by offering participation in cutting-edge projects. If you are visiting your homeland of Ireland, you may visit a job fair held to attract the Irish diaspora. If you are from Singapore, you could receive a bonus if you decide to come home. Such campaigns are evident around the world, from Zurich to Paris, to Frankfurt, to Hong Kong, to Tokyo.

Those US firms that recruited from abroad obviously aren't happy with this development. Nor are they pleased that other countries are not only looking to bring home their nationals but to entice US nationals.

THE SEARCH FOR "AMERICANIZED EUROPEANS"

Not that being an American executive is the first choice for every country. European companies prefer their top executives to be from Europe, according to Sharon Voros, author of *Leadership Presence* (Adams Media, 1999) and *the Road to CEO* (Adams Media, 2000); the most desirable of candidates are "Americanized Europeans;" that is, Europeans with MBAs from Wharton, Harvard, or some other prestigious US graduate school and job time with a firm like McKinsey & Co. or Bain. Said Don Utroska, a partner with Chicago recruiter Dieckmann & Associates, "Companies don't want to risk losing revenues and customers, and they feel Americans are less attuned to cultural issues and local customs."

IT personnel are another story. European companies are desperately in search for some kinds of workers, IT personnel to begin with and then specialists in international finance, marketing and law. "Worker bees of the global information age" is how Shailagh Murray refers to them, writing in *The Wall Street Journal* about the high-tech labor shortage in Europe attracting American headhunters. According to a study by the International Data Corporation, Western Europe is suffering from such a shortage of people with information technology skills that almost half a million full-time jobs stand unfilled – and this figure could more than triple to 1.6 million by the end of 2002.

AUSTRALIA'S GLOBAL RECRUITMENT EFFORTS

Last year the Australian Information Industry Association, with its nation's Department of Immigration, met with national companies to remind them that their country has fewer pre-conditions and restrictions on immigration than countries like Germany and Singapore with their annual visa quotas. An AIIA spokesperson reminds, "Australia provides unrestricted work rights to the spouses of IT workers with temporary entry visas." Further, Australia allows local companies to hire overseas students studying IT in Australia once they finish their degrees.

At the same time, Australian firms are doing their utmost to retain their employees. A study by Mercer Cullen Egan Dell found that 84% of organizations surveyed in 1999 offered some form of flexible work practice, up from 56% in 1998 and 32% in 1995 to increase their organization's attractiveness as an "employer of choice." Mercer Cullen Egan Dell's HR information services team leader Merrilyn Earl said, "Employers have to be able to tailor working arrangements to suit the needs of their key individuals - or risk losing them."

Likewise, Asian companies are concerned about keeping their own employees while attracting talent from abroad.

All along, exchange of talent between Europe and America has occurred. But as industry in Asia grows, it, too, will need to create a marketplace for recruitment firms seeking talent from abroad to prosper. Dunhill Management Services, Victoria, is one of the new players in the Asia Pacific, according to Cliff Stoneman, its director. Says Stoneman, "The Asian marketplace is being forced more and more to compete aggressively for skilled professionals on the global stage. In the coming years, we will see the Asia Pacific region battle against the United States and Europe to lure and retain the best people." Success against other countries, however, will require firms in the region to offer the kinds of financial incentives comparable to that gained elsewhere. Only then can global recruiters do their task of attracting and relocating the right people.

These right people will need not only the necessary skills, but also the capability to fit easily in different cultures.

ONLINE RECRUITMENT

As competition becomes global, however, countries that create a climate for recruitment must expect that interest will go both ways. Take Thailand. Online job seeking services are growing there as international job recruitment agencies see a gap in the recruitment market. At least three overseas online job recruitment companies exist there, including the German company Jobs and Adverts AG, which has a branch in Thailand to provide online job recruitment on its Website (www.jobpilot.co.th). But just as this online service should help in local recruitment and recruitment abroad, it may also allow Thai workers to apply to companies around the world without having to pay fees to third parties.

According to Suchada Sukhsawat Na Ayutthaya, president of the Personnel Management Association of Thailand, online recruitment technology's popularity seems to be growing as quickly in Thailand as it did in the US. Jobs and Adverts' Website is already six years old and covers more than 13 Asian countries. Its database holds thousands of résumés, and its corporate customers include BMW (Thailand), Coca-Cola Services Ltd, and Unilever Thai Holdings Ltd. Traffic is in the tens of thousands.

Posting a résumé is seen as sending a message to prospective employers that you are familiar with the new technology.

VIRTUAL INTERVIEWS

In the future, besides "resumails," as they are called among the Thai, job seekers and employers may be able to use videoconferencing for purposes of recruitment. Such technology certainly would represent a financial saving for prospective employees who might otherwise have to travel overseas for a job interview. In essence, interviewers would conduct a "virtual interview" with applicants. Videoconferencing has certainly proven helpful for US recruiters. The US has already begun to use this technology to put American employers in touch with candidates in London, Toronto, Vancouver, Bombay, and Tel Aviv.

In the more industrialized parts of the world, international recruitment companies like Korn/Ferry and Heidrick & Struggles International Inc. can be found practicing their trade. Smaller firms have found that they need to band together to form a network like the World Search Group with 18 small executive search firms. The giants in global recruiting can leverage client contacts and manpower across borders through their global network in a way the independents can't without such structure.

Staff at recruitment firms locally reflect the hiring trends in their area. So, for instance, Korn/Ferry International laid off 10% of its North American staff while projecting a 15% increase in China.

US ECONOMIC SLOWDOWN

Despite the economic slowdown in the US, a study by online immigration services provider VisaNow.com has found that the demand by US companies to hire skilled foreign workers is at its highest level ever. "Even with reports of large-scale layoffs in the tech industry, unemployment rates in the US are still relatively low. There are tens, maybe hundreds of thousands of jobs that companies cannot fill due to a lack of available American workers," says Robert C. Meltzer, president of VisaNow.com. "It isn't just the IT industry but in aerospace, biotech, engineering, and healthcare. All of these sectors look to hire H-1B workers when the domestic talent pool runs dry."

Two reports back Meltzer's assertion. An April 2001 study by the IT Association of America revealed that 425,000 IT positions will go unfilled in the US this year due to a lack of candidates with requisite skills. And in June 2001 the Meta Group reported that despite the dotcom bust, US companies are still struggling to fill as many as 600,000 IT positions.

Headlines about the state of the US economy may be misleading those abroad, opening the door for the Europeans to recruit more actively in areas where the US was very active – like India. Recruitment of Indian IT staff is set to double in 2001 as British firms take advantage of the slowdown in demand from the US and relaxed entry rules. In March 2001, more than 21,000 work permits had been issued to Indian nationals. A major resource for IT employees, India overtook the US to become the top country for issue of work permits at the start of the new millennium.

Of course, this has raised concerns in India among local companies that worry that the relaxation of the rules and introduction of fast-track permits for certain IT staff by the UK, including IT managers, business analysts, and network staff might lead to a skills shortage of their own. Concerned about retaining talented workers, business leaders there are implementing programs from more industrialized countries. For instance, the Indian mutual fund industry is beginning to use employee stock option programs to attract and hold key personnel.

According to Derek A. Langley, president and CEO of global services company Hexaware Technologies, and a senior member of the Computing Services and Software Association, interest from the

UK in India as a resource stems from the estimated shortage of almost 200,000 software engineers in the UK. British firms are finding an increasing talent pool in India, however, as hundreds of IT workers, laid off from contracts in the US, return to the Indian job market only to find fewer jobs than in the past. According to CRV Consultants, one of Bangalore's biggest headhunting firms, the situation reflects a dramatic turnaround from 2000, when applicants had their choice of employer. There has been a 20% falloff in recruitment to fill only a few specific jobs. Firms haven't stopped hiring; they are just less aggressive. Sun Microsystems in India, for instance, told reporters it has "gone slow" on recruitment. UK firms that are recruiting within the India labor pool are especially interested in prospects who previously worked in the US, and consequently are familiar with western working conditions. But this doesn't mean it is simple for them to find work in the UK. They must get an entry visa from the British High Commission to come to the UK to be interviewed, then return to India to receive a work permit. And if the job involves more than six months' work, they need to get medical clearance, a two-week procedure.

Not easy? In the past, the situation was more onerous. UK companies had to prove that they were unable to find suitable staff in the UK before they looked overseas for employees. Which meant UK firms often couldn't even begin to recruit for several months, let alone bring suitable overseas candidates into the UK. The consequence: important IT projects were delayed, a serious competitive disadvantage. Today, in e-commerce time, each week is the equivalent of a year in terms of lost opportunity.

British companies using overseas IT services firms also had difficulties. Offshore consultants had to wait weeks for permission to visit the UK to assess, cost, and plan software projects.

THE PEOPLE AND ADMINISTRATIVE ISSUES

It still isn't easy recruiting from another country. It is a major commitment, not only by the employee, but also by the overseas employer. Apart from relocation costs, there may be language questions and businesses will have to look after employees when it comes to finding somewhere to live and getting transport. All this makes for high administrative costs – and is even more costly if the transplanted employee fails.

Past experience in relocating employees has shown how making a global move can be easier on some than on others. Or, said another way, getting a flat tire fixed may be relatively easy in your home town, but having it done when you are away isn't as easy, and can be awful for some people if they have to get it done in a foreign country. Lack of knowledge of the local environment can be confusing and very frustrating, more so for some people than others, and increases the time it takes for expatriates to adapt, ultimately costing the new employer. But there is also culture shock on a personal level; that is, in terms of expectations in relation to corporate climate and objectives. There may be a mismatch, which ultimately leads to the individual's return to his or her native soil. This is as applicable if you are reassigning a current employee as recruiting from a distant country.

RETAINING GLOBAL RECRUITS

Assuming that you have recruited from abroad, how do you keep them on staff, assuming they take well to the new country? According to a survey by Mercer Management Consulting, the regional labor market, economic climate, competition, and attractiveness of the locale – all influence the quantity, quality and enthusiasm of prospective new hires. Likewise, all the programs, policies, and practices that make up the "work climate," not to mention compensation and benefits, business strategy, and flexibility and autonomy of a job, determine an enterprise's ability to keep someone's interest. Finally, employees have values and interests that can determine whether they join or stray to another company in the country.

ADVICE FOR GLOBAL RECRUITERS

If you can't find the talent you want in your own country, there are recruitment firms and Internet Websites that will enable you to look beyond your nation's borders. Likewise, these same resources can help you people overseas operations with nationals rather than use expatriates to staff them. Whether you use an international headhunter like Korn/Ferry International Inc. or a Website that specializes in overseas jobs like Overseas

Jobs Express (www.overseasjobs.com), which lists entry level to senior executive posts, your description of the job will influence the response you get from talented employees to your job opening. Here is what Peter D. Weddle, publisher of *Weddle's*, the newsletter about online recruitment, suggests that you talk about.

Challenging work

Stay away from a list of requirements and responsibilities. Instead, describe the opening from an applicant's perspective. So talk about the opportunities that the job will offer for the holder to be involved in important and meaningful work. Discuss the corporate mission and the value of that mission and then describe how the job holder will contribute to achievement of the mission.

Personal development

Yes, you will provide opportunities for additional training but that is expected, particularly if the job is in the IT area. The candidate is looking for development beyond that; that is, professional development that comes from an opportunity to be mentored by leaders in the organization and to participate in key decisions that impact the success of the company. Still, do mention if the company will subsidize higher education degrees and support involvement in professional associations.

Advancement

Demonstrate that there are opportunities for upward mobility in your organization by posting examples on your own Website. This should catch the attention of foreign nationals willing to relocate to build their career. Let those hired to represent your firm abroad know, too, about specific examples of personal advancement within your company, ideally by others recruited abroad.

Collegial relationships

Let executive recruiters know about other superstars on your management team so they can mention them to prospective candidates. On your Website, play up these individuals. Says Weddle, "Include their picture and a description of their work, in their own words." Update the site regularly with new profiles; you want prospective employees to see that your organization isn't limited to one or two "names."

Support/resources

If you will be relocating a manager and family, you want to be sure that services are available to help them make the transition – physical and cultural. At the very least help them locate a home, even for the short term, and a local school for any children. Provide training in the language and career placement assistance for the spouse if that is an issue of interest. Depending on the position, mention should also be made about workplace resources like special computer systems, access to technical libraries or data, or information on new research that can make relocation seem worthwhile.

Compensation

"Competitive salary" or "salary commensurate with skills and experience," says Weddle, will mean little to someone coming from another country, particularly someone whom you truly need on your staff. Don't try to pay less because you are recruiting from a developing country. It will take little time for a new hire to understand how he or she stands financially to peers. If the pay and benefits aren't comparable to that of colleagues, you are likely to lose your new hire to another firm quickly. Better to talk about stock options and base plus incentive early in the recruitment process. Certainly include that information in any international Internet postings. As Weddle's research has found, salary information must appear in the first five lines of a job posting or most candidates will read no further. What about staffing overseas subsidiaries with nationals? The same rule applies. Big distinctions found between expatriate and local national pay, benefits, and bonuses can encourage the brightest local nationals to learn as much as they can from you, then move on.

The State of the Art of Recruitment and Retention

The war for talent began during the boom days. Despite the wishes of managers, the problem is likely to continue through the economic downturn. Those with the ability to go elsewhere likely will do so if they don't feel their jobs are secure or are dissatisfied with the current work environment. This chapter identifies those elements that created recruitment and retention problems during the boom days and will continue to impact attrition even more during the economic downturn. Find out how the following stack up in today's job market.

» Pay and benefits.
» Career development opportunities.
» Corporate reputation – including reputation for financial soundness, quality work, management capability, and social consciousness.
» Employee empowerment.
» Access to the dollars and other resources to get the job done.

As I write this report on the state of recruitment and retention, the situation has changed dramatically from only a few months before. Generally, the state of the world economy is guarded. In some countries, like the US, the "r" word – "recession" – is an accepted fact, no longer a whisper. Other countries' economies have begun to spiral downward or business leaders are showing serious concern about the near future. What can we expect to happen to the management issue of recruitment and retention if the economic boom becomes bust where we are located? Will the competition for talented employees be over?

Not at all. Uncertain economic times can undermine productivity, focus, and morale – at a time when companies are most reliant on the best efforts of key people. In addition, the economic downturn may prompt some valued employees to rethink their current situations – particularly employees whose compensation packages emphasize stock options, which now may be "under water." According to HayGroup, times of economic change and upheaval are when it's critical to really listen to valued employees – even if the instinct is to focus more on strategy and cost control than on personnel.

With downsizings occurring, is there a shortage of people? Good people, yes. A recent survey by the American Management Association found that about 40% of respondent firms still had plans to create new jobs in the coming 12 months. Further, when asked about available talent, 46.7% used the term "scarce" rather than either "abundant" or "adequate" to describe the situation. While this is an improvement over an earlier survey in which 75.6% of respondents used the term "scarce" to describe the talented employees they needed, the issue seems not to be about warm bodies to fill lots of new and existing jobs, but rather skilled and high performers to fill critical positions – from high-tech to retail and sales to skilled managerial spots. In the US, for one, the ranks of unemployed have yet to reach 5% of the population, which statisticians claim would mean a shift in job market from one controlled by the sellers (employees) to one determined by the buyers (employers).

So the situation is statistically very different from only a few years before. In the late 1990s, companies were scrambling to hire and retain the people they needed. Companies offered large signing bonuses. Employees demanded raises only a few months after they had been hired. And headhunters sought out talented IT and other managers in short supply before they had yet decorated their new office with a better offer from another employer. Depending on their background and expertise, employees as well as managers pretty much were in the cat bird's seat about where they wanted to work. Remember when many young high-tech firms had hundreds of vacancies they couldn't fill, and more conservative banks and consulting firms were losing talent to these upstarts, dot-coms, and other companies on high-growth tracks. For one, McKinsey & Company's "War for talent" survey, updated in 2000, found 99% of the responding corporations were concerned about their current managerial pools. Only 20% agreed that they had enough talent to pursue most of their companies' business opportunities.

A national survey by Kepner-Tregoe, Inc. in 1999 reported that "competition for experienced, talented workers would likely continue, if not intensify, as we entered the new millennium." Further, said K-T, mobility in the workforce had reached an all-time high. In the survey 60% of the 1,290 respondents admitted that they themselves think about leaving their job one to two times a year or more. More than 60% of both managers and workers reported co-workers frequently discussed leaving. Turnover in established companies was said to be around 6% while in new companies – which included high-tech communications and computer firms – it was as high as 30 to 40%. Among those with technology backgrounds, according to a study by the US Bureau of Labor Statistics, job-hopping has become an obsession and "they never stop job hunting."

The July/August 1998 issue of *Across the Board* suggested that organizations were spending an average of $30,000 to $50,000 per new hire, including the money not only for recruitment, but also training and lost productivity during the learning curve. Because of a booming economy, there was opportunity for growth, but money that could be spent to expand the business had to be invested, instead, in replacing employees. This didn't even reflect the "soft" costs; that is, lost intellectual capital as seasoned employees took intimate knowledge of the workings of the organization with them as they left; sluggish product development from lost ideas and market knowledge; sudden holes in succession plans; lost competitive advantage as employees joined competitors; and decreased morale and increased stress among remaining employees.

Given the impact of turnover on immediate savings and increased long-term growth, it was inevitable that companies would hold focus groups and "town meetings" and conduct employee surveys to determine how to stem the tide of turnover. Subsequent actions ranged from changes in payroll and benefits to make them more competitive to more flexible work schedules, to increased on-the-job training, to more defined career paths, to concierge and other services to meet personal needs. How did these initiatives fare? For one, money wasn't perceived to be a deciding factor, according to the K-T survey. Even among technical personnel, it played little part in putting an end to job hopping, according to a ComputerWorld survey of 500 IT professionals that showed that "they would trade a big bonus for flextime, greater intellectual challenge, and training."

On the other extreme, concierge services also played little part in increasing retention. Meant to communicate that management cared about its people, they were perceived as perks and nothing more. The results of studies at the time reflected that employee treatment was the key reason why employees did not stay, thereby supporting the ongoing work of Robert Levering and Milton Moskowitz reported in their groundbreaking best-seller *The 100 Best Companies to Work for in America*, first published in 1994 and updated annually in *Fortune* magazine. Take the National Employee Relationship Report, a 1999 survey of US companies co-sponsored by Walker Information, Inc. and the Hudson Institute. The study found these six factors influenced the decision to stay beyond two years.

» Fairness at work: fair pay, performance evaluations, and corporate policies.
» Care and concern: career development opportunities and family-friendly benefits.
» Satisfaction with day-to-day activities.
» Corporate reputation: an employer with a strong, capable management team is financially sound, and does high-quality work.
» Trust in employees: freedom of employees to make decisions, manage their own time, control resources, and test new ideas.
» Work and job resources: the people and equipment to do the work.

Employees want open communication between themselves and management and the opportunity to gain new skills. They also want work that is fun, interesting, and exciting. In addition, many of today's workers want to work in an environment with leading-edge technology. Executives rank high in worth company values and culture, autonomy, and a well-managed company. It isn't a single program or initiative that can keep an employee with a company, albeit they can interest job candidates to apply to a job opening. Rather, it is satisfaction with the job, supervision, culture and climate, and opportunity for professional growth through training and advancement.

Given all the studies during the recruitment/retention crisis of the boom years, it would seem natural that companies learned much about how to recruit for tough-to-fill positions and also how to become an "employer of choice," a company likely to retain employees. While past experience may have taught companies about new avenues to reach potential recruits and even techniques to increase the likelihood of selecting good performers, retention may continue to be a problem, even in these gray economic times.

Companies learned to find new hires in unlikely places. They held job fairs in colleges to get entry-level employees and went to the armed services to recruit retirees for management and technical positions requiring more job experience. They recruited from abroad and from immigrant groups within their company. They checked business headlines for major changes, like mergers and acquisitions, and checked for talented managers who might be prepared to move to a more secure position elsewhere. Many companies learned to recruit continuously, to create a pool of pre-selected, visible candidates. Yes, this often meant a more active role for HR professionals, attending trade conferences and meetings, calling article authors and subjects profiled in articles, and members of local/regional/national trade groups, but it ensured talented individuals ready to step in when a vacancy occurred.

As brick and mortar firms built Websites, those sites became representative of the firms and were used not only to attract customers, but also to entice job candidates – both those looking for work and passive job seekers who might consider the company for employment – particularly IT personnel. Sites like those maintained by Dell and Mitsubishi play up the training opportunities and positive work culture on their homepages. There were fewer traditional advertisements in trade magazines and newspapers and more advertisements on the Web at designated sites like headhunter.net, an approach that guaranteed more people would see the ads, larger numbers of returns, and speedier placement of a candidate. Referrals also proved to be an effective way to get new hires, and the high performance records of those who were hired that way contributed to its increase in use.

Companies came up with dollars and awards to employees who brought in suitable candidates. It would seem to be a great scheme for individuals to get rid of an unemployed uncle or friend who was borrowing money, but history has shown that those who made referrals were very particular about the people they brought to their companies. They saw their reputation at stake if they brought to the attention of the company someone less than hard working. Besides, who would want a "loser" on the payroll, someone you brought into the company and whose poor work performance you now must cover for, day in and day out?

Companies also have moved beyond hiring based on requirements specified in job descriptions. Increasingly, companies are using competency-based recruitment to ensure that the skills, abilities, knowledge, and attitudes of best performers in a job are replicated in candidates for consideration in a similar job. Companies have found that hard skills can be developed with training, but softer skills (competencies) aren't so easily developed in employees. Better to find them during the recruitment process. Employers who were frustrated with the need to continually rehire for the same position may have scoffed at first at the idea of taking the time to uncover the competencies of superior performers in high-turnover positions, but the real-time experience soon showed them that to do otherwise was to condemn their firm to an endless cycle of rehiring and retraining.

The ideal program involves interviews with both outstanding performers and mediocre or average workers in which critical work situations are described and each group is asked how they would address the matter. In time, those skills, abilities, knowledge, and attitudes that differentiate the two groups become clear. They, then, become the requirements or qualifications for prospective candidates for the job, increasing the odds of hiring a good performer in the job – and decreasing the likelihood of turnover from mismatch between skills and job.

New hire turnover is the most expensive turnover of all, because the organization reaps no benefits from the new hire, only all the costs of recruiting. Given the high turnover in the recent past, companies have been looking for ways to reduce the number of false starts. There are many factors over which HR professionals have no control, such as counteroffers or interview offers from other employers, but they have identified some creative techniques to reduce mismatch between a job as described and a job as experienced. For instance, job simulations during the interview process help to "screen in" candidates who perform well but do not interview well. Further, what you see, hear, and experience during the interview eliminate any misconceptions about the job. This may be why simulations have come to be used in recruitment of high-turnover positions, such as in customer service, IT, telemarketing, and the like.

The secret to success of such simulations is the replication to the real job. For this to happen, the top performers of the job are questioned about their activities, in particular the most challenging. Information is gathered to provide candidates with a realistic glimpse of the day-to-day activities required to be successful in the job. Different techniques then are used to imitate the work situation. Most often, job prospects are given real work assignments, sometimes work demanding a full day of test-driving the job to determine their capability and comfort level with the position. Rather than the real job, some candidates are asked to complete "inbox exercises," solving problems or making decisions, or handling paperwork, typical of what they might have to handle in the course of their work. If running a meeting is critical to the success of a job holder (e.g., a project leader), the simulation might be to lead a meeting and facilitate the discussion.

If a candidate is one an organization wants but he or she is unsure about the fit, the organization might propose a process called "job shadowing," in which the favored candidate spends time shadowing the current occupant of the position to fully understand the range of job responsibilities.

So companies worked to reduce turnover from poor job matches, and for this purpose, too, conducted exit interviews as employees left, although the worth of reasons given is problematic. While substantial information may be garnered from an exit interview, the desire for a positive reference may minimize an employee's willingness to talk about the real factors in the decision to leave. Which explains the substantial research in the area of turnover during the boom years and continued research since the economic downturn to determine likely attrition rates in poor times.

Evidence suggests that there are reasons why new hires leave just when they are getting started and, frequently bewildering, sometimes never show up for work at all. After accepting a job offer with a new employer, the new hire announces his or her intention to the current employer and receives a counteroffer. The offer may take the form of a promise for career advancement or flextime, a retention bonus, or some change in the current work assignment. Since considerable time and money may have been invested in making the hiring decision, companies have learned to talk openly about the possibility of counteroffers and ask newly hired individuals to resist them. Another possibility: another job offer from another employer that is better than the one accepted. Individuals seeking a new job will often generate multiple offers, one after the other. Even if the employee accepts one, if another offer comes through, he or she may choose to accept this later one for any of a number of reasons – from the nature of the work, to the compensation, to the location of the firm. Whatever the circumstances, recruiters need to be alert to this possibility and preclude its occurrence by attempting to uncover any outstanding needs so that a competing job offer is likely to be declined.

The first few weeks on the job may also raise questions in a new hire's mind about the decision to work for a firm. The orientation program itself may be at fault. The individual may not feel welcome or feel that those around him or her will be supportive. Maybe there was a promise about further training and nothing is mentioned about it during the orientation. While the new technology enables more communication, information that will orient the new hire to the organization might better be communicated in person than via the corporate intranet.

The job itself may also fall short of the promised challenge. If the company hasn't gone out of its way to ensure that the employee understands the work he or she will be doing, then there may be a big enough mismatch that the employee quietly undertakes another job search after a week or so on the new job. The likelihood of this situation can be reduced via simulation or job shadowing or other real-world experience with the job during the recruitment process.

But there are other promises made during recruitment that, proven false, can trigger new hires to restart their job search. They are broken promises about training opportunities or work culture or management style. Which brings us to an assortment of problems that can contribute to high turnover among mobile employees or tough-to-hire positions regardless of economic conditions. Many of the same factors that were behind turnover during boom years can contribute to high attrition in critical positions during a downturn. Indeed, a major factor began in the previous economic downturn: lack of corporate loyalty.

Beginning in the late 1980s, as companies began to downsize to reduce expenses, employees got the message that "everyone is dispensable." Doing a good job offered no guarantees. Anyone, anytime, anywhere could be axed. And those terminated could readily be replaced by others because labor was plentiful. Retention wasn't a goal, so companies cut benefits, training, and opportunities for advancement. As we moved into the recession of the early 1990s, companies put responsibility for career growth and development squarely on the shoulders of their employees. Yes, the company would provide the training, but employees were in charge of their own careers. There was a new social covenant, one that seemed to reflect the belief of management that employees were, indeed, a competitive advantage, but they also were an expendable commodity whose work could be outsourced. Employee loyalty no longer guaranteed lifetime job security. No matter your contribution to the bottom line, your position was not a given. If you were to ensure job security, you had to do it on your own, even if it meant moving to another employer. The consequences of the slash-and-burn business practices of the 1980s and early 1990s can be found in this quotation from Peter Drucker:

> "All organizations now say routinely, 'People are our greatest asset.' Yet few practice what they preach, let alone truly believe it. Most still believe, though perhaps not consciously, what nineteenth-century employers believed: People need us more than

we need them. But, in fact, organizations have to market member-ship as much as they market products and services – and perhaps more. They have to attract people, hold people, recognize and reward people, motivate people, and serve and satisfy people."

So, in today's downward spiraling economy, we come to the same "people" issue that triggered in part the employee retention problem of the boom years. The fear of layoff draws people's attention away from innovation and productivity to their own safety and careers, away from the success of the organization to their own security. The full ramifications of high employee attrition may be more evident in today's economy than in the previous boom years. During the economic boom, as HR managers pointed to the high point of employee turnover, they focused on the costs of recruitment, training, lost productivity when new and inexperienced employees replace older ones. Little was said about lost product and market ideas and lost market share given the relationship between employee retention and customer acquisition and retention. Yet these consequences are critical to corporate success – and will be even more so if the economic downturn stays awhile.

So there would seem to be a need for a high-loyalty people strategy to discourage turnover, certainly of the most talented within the organization. Hay Consulting sees the need for a new covenant, one that promises employees the tools to help them grow and advance *because they care about their employees' career growth*. "It is not enough merely to say, 'We care,' although it never hurts to do so. Companies must back up that message with initiatives that make employees feel their current job is the best path to achieving their career goals," as the Hay study concludes. The first step is to identify problems within the culture, work relationships between employees and supervisors, and compensation and benefits programs, respect for senior management, and professed opportunities to grow and advance. Just as companies at this juncture in time need to assess market strategy and product performance, they need to survey the commitment and enthusiasm of their best people.

A study by Hay in the early 1990s identified three factors of importance: partnership or involvement of employees in decisions, employability or opportunity to ensure career security if not job security, and cafeteria-styled compensation and benefits programs. A more recent study by the consulting firm identified some factors of importance to employees worthy of further investigation within each company.

» Employees want a competent leader with a game plan – not just a "nice person" in charge. Hay points out that three-quarters of unhappy employees do not believe their company knows where it is going, too often untrue. So all that may be needed to change this perception is a strong communication effort.

» A bigger challenge than attrition during tight economic times may be "mental attrition" in which employees, unable to leave their jobs, "tune out" or find other ways to avoid work (e.g., absenteeism, frequent sick leave). Those employees who shirk their responsibility only burden their teammates with additional responsibility. They should be let go.

» Employee training and development programs mean little to employees if they aren't given the chance to practice the knowledge and skills they have acquired from them. So training needs to be relevant and it needs to be used to broaden experience. High achievers need positions that provide stretch. Such opportunity will give them reason to stay around. Says Hay, "Cross-functional moves, profit-and-loss responsibility, the chance to start a new business activity, participation in a high-profile task force, and even temporary assignments – all these place employees in unfamiliar territory where they can develop new skills and grow."

» Compensation is less a factor in retention and more in recruitment; that is, employees are less likely to look for a job because of their compensation, but more likely to accept a job offer based on the level of compensation offered.

» Compensation is not an issue within the high-tech industry; rather, retention is highest among companies that are most successful in accommodating employees' work/life balance.

The findings of the Hay study, done on the brink of the economic downturn in the US, mirrors very closely findings of other studies done in the midst of an economic boom. Good performers were found to leave because they saw no link between their pay and performance. They complained that there was no growth or advancement opportunities, their work was not seen as important, nor were their contributions recognized and valued by others. They weren't able to use their natural talents. And they were often supervised by managers who created "toxic work environments."

If we look to satisfy these demands by employees and thereby reduce turnover, we see a new approach to recruitment and retention, a strategic approach to staffing rather than a program-oriented one. Recruitment and retention and those elements that promote success with both should be as much a part of the company's strategic plan as product introductions and marketing campaigns. As part of that people side of the plan should be aggressive and resourceful recruitment; the ideal, as evident by current trends, is to develop a pool of talent from which you can identify outstanding prospects as the needs arise.

Training should lead somewhere. People's personal concerns should be kept in mind, no matter how lean the organization, to ensure work/family balance.

To keep your most talented employees, you need to create a healthy, dynamic culture. And the formula for that would also be within the strategic plan dedicated to people management. Positive cultures take their cue from senior management, and it will be senior management's responsibility to support initiatives that transform the work environment and work relationships between managers and employees into the productive ones they should be.

In Practice

If you consider the practices of companies with low turnover rates, you find that key to high retention is focus on the people, not on the issue of retention. This chapter looks at some companies with low turnover rates because they have built people programs around a set of core values that have been found to be critical to most talented personnel. Read about:

» The US Army
» Steelcase
» AlliedSignal
» General Electric.

Some businesses need to increase their public visibility to interest job candidates. They may have programs within their organizations that were instituted to help employees or address social or community issues, but their presence may make prospective hires proud to work for them. A good PR campaign that publicizes these initiatives may be all these firms need to increase the number of prospective hires at their doors. This tactic is particularly beneficial for smaller organizations, but large companies shouldn't ignore the marketing value, either.

What kinds of programs am I suggesting that should be publicized?

There are programs like the childcare program that BankBoston offers its employees on snowy days. While such a perk might seem insignificant, this free service is important enough to the 16,000 employees who work at the seven BankBoston locations in Massachusetts, Rhode Island, and Connecticut to keep turnover low. Imagine how notice in the press might draw single parents.

Then there are companies that demonstrate social consciousness. For employees who are like minded, they might be interested in applying for work at a firm like Brink's Home Security that gives one day off per employee per year, in every office, to volunteer in community service. Brink's isn't alone in doing this, either. Another example: Timberland employees may use up to 40 hours of paid time per year for volunteer work. Not only do programs like these stimulate interest in the companies, but they also discourage those already employed at them from considering a move elsewhere.

Corporate social consciousness need not end at the borders of the city or country. The Body Shop, a retailer of bath and beauty supplies, for instance, has found its efforts in disadvantaged parts of the world to help others, as well as its ethical culture, has enabled it to attract and retain employees – and even encourage part-timers to return year after year during the December holidays.

Studies show that today's employees want to grow in their jobs. So educational programs like those offered by CIGNA Group Insurance in Philadelphia also can interest prospective employees, as well as make current employees deaf to a recruitment agent from a competitive firm. Like most firms, CIGNA has an education reimbursement program that pays for employees who have completed undergraduate degrees to get advanced degrees. But more significant is the program sponsored by CIGNA that allows employees to earn an undergraduate liberal arts degree from the University of Pennsylvania without ever having to leave the workplace.

Brought to the attention of the press, such a program makes a good story. But it also would interest parents with minimal time to attend college at night or the resources to pay for added education. Certainly it has contributed to employee retention. According to the Workforce Stability Institute's CEO Roger Herman, 97% of the graduates of the program have remained with the company.

Programs that demonstrate an awareness of the work/family issues that face employees certainly are worth getting press coverage for the benefit they can give to the recruitment practice. Reminding employees about the existence of such programs can also reduce turnover. Take the efforts at SAS, the largest privately held software company in the world, with turnover of less than 4% in Silicon Valley, where the average rate is 25%. This represents a savings of $70mn each year in employee replacement costs. SAS attributes its stellar record to its on-site daycare, on-site recreational facilities, and most important its 35-hour workweek.

Some individuals want to work in an environment of innovation or teamwork. So stories about initiatives that promote these cultural issues also benefit recruitment, if not retention, as current employees are reminded about what they have. At London-based Ideo, an international product design firm with offices in the US, Munich, Tokyo, and Tel Aviv, applicants have to prove their worthiness to work for the firm with a long and drawn out recruitment process. There are three or four interviews with staff. Candidates show and discuss their work with a group of Ideo people who, in turn, acquaint them with projects under way at the company. "We spend a lot of time talking to people and thinking about how they'll fit," recruiting coordinator Colin Burns says. "The personality thing is important because we rely on each other. It's a human business and you have to know how to work together and respect each other. People who are egotistical won't make it."

If you visit the Website for Fujitsu Limited's Australian and New Zealand subsidiaries, you gain insight into its appeal to people's desire to grow professionally yet work collegially. The copy reads, "We believe that the success of the modern corporation is directly aligned to the creativity and imagination of its people – and we're committed to providing an environment and a developmental scheme that will allow people to truly realize their potential in these areas." Fujitsu offers situational training to fine-tune communication and consulting skills. Graduates of the program undergo individual assessments and receive extensive technical training.

While the purpose of these programs may not have been to demonstrate that its creator was an "employer of choice," they may say that to many who hear about them. People go to work for a company that offers programs that make their personal lives better, do good works for the community or the world at large, or provide professional growth.

If you want such initiatives to help with recruitment, note the following.

» Alert local newspapers and TV stations about programs that range from *pro bono* projects to fun events. Media publicity not only spreads word about your business to the world at large, but serves to validate to current employees that the organization is a great place in which to work.

» Since the opportunity to increase employability has been found to influence recruitment and retention, make mention of training opportunities for employees to recruiters and in print and online advertisements. In corporate newsletters and on the intranet, don't forget to remind employees of this benefit to employment with your firm. Your current employees might be considering moving to another firm for the same kind of training your firm already offers.

» Include information about these events and projects on your Internet site if you have pages devoted to recruitment – which you should have. Such stories on your Website lets job hunters know that your company is a great place to work.

» Develop brochures that promote the best qualities of your organization if you get regular inquiries about working for your firm. Don't limit yourself to your corporate annual report and shareholder reports. Harvard University, for instance, has created a brochure with a picturesque, aerial view of the campus and copy that describes the school as one with "small, collaborative work groups, each with its own personality and goals." In other words, Harvard isn't the big, impersonal institution you might have thought it was. Rather, it is a community of educators who will get generous vacation time, free attendance to Harvard courses, wellness programs, and a university-funded retirement plan.

What makes these programs beneficial is that they address issues that are attractive to talented individuals:

» the opportunity to increase employability through training;
» pride in one's organization's products or services to the community or world at large;
» respect for employees' personal needs as well as professional contributions; and
» a culture of teamwork and innovation.

ASK UNCLE SAM

The US Armed Services may seem a strange example to place before corporations around the world as a recruitment model, but the US Army, Navy, Air Force, Marines, and Coast Guard have the same recruitment challenges as other organizations, and they have learned how to adapt their recruitment tactics to attract recruits since the end of the draft. Yes, there continue to be Armed Forces recruitment offices located in almost every mid-sized city and most towns, but today the Armed Services also has a personalized Website with links to specific branches of the Services. All right, your organization can't afford the various recruitment offices or major marketing campaigns on television (like the Armed Services "Be all that you can be"), but what about a Website that tells you "Each year, the Military hires over 365,000 new enlisted and office personnel, so opportunities (technical and non-technical) are always plentiful. The five Services offer over 300 schools and 10,000 courses of instruction. This free training, and the experience that follows, gives the Military veteran a real advantage in the civilian world."

In other words, not only are the opportunities to learn in a job in the Military many, but so are the opportunities for future advancement – a message that might be considered by corporations, since it could make even a lateral move to a new employer seem of interest to a prospective employee.

Let's focus on the US Army. What practices should organizations adapt to their situations? Some organizations have already found practices of the Army worth emulation, some may be new to most companies but worth consideration. The recruitment effort does all the following.

» **Profiles enlistment candidates**. The Army knows both what make good enlistees and what interests prospective enlistees, and it uses such information in its recruitment strategies. Once again, if you visit the US Army's Website, copy talks about "challenging career opportunities," "a lifetime of security," "excitement," and "families." There is mention that soldiers work as a "team," and that today's "Army of Excellence" offers an opportunity for men and women to work on "highly technical electronic systems."

» **Keeps track of prospective candidates**. Since recruitment is a continuous process, the Army keeps track of those candidates who considered the Armed Services but then declined the opportunity. It is somewhat influenced by the recruiter's personal style, but Army recruiters are taught to flag occupations or benefits that interest interviewed candidates and, then, about three months after the contact, follow up with a personal note or even an applicable brochure or update. Only after the prospect truly turns down the opportunity does further correspondence end.

» **Develops targeted recruitment brochures**. The Army routinely prints full-color recruitment brochures that reflect segment marketing, with different brochures based on different interests (e.g., travel or an opportunity to work with the latest technology). The brochures are even segmented by population, such as women, people of color, or potential enlistees who have families.

» **Rewards for referrals**. The rewards vary, from such simple things as specialized jackets to a promotion in rank, including a pay raise, depending on the number of successful referrals. This might seem unusual for the Army, but it is a popular practice in many companies. For one, Deloitte & Touche will pay as much as $10,000 for referrals for hard-to-fill promotions and trips for two abroad. There is a reason for these payments. Companies have found that referred employees stay longer with the organization (Deloitte & Touche report 33% longer), and candidates referred by those within the organization – whether the Military or corporation – are usually a better fit. Those who make the referral have a better sense of what the organization needs, and consequently refer friends or relatives they know are likely to fit the culture or climate of the organization.

Incidentally, this isn't only a US practice. The Ireland-based Analog Devices offers $2000 bounty for those who help them find skilled engineers and other critical staff. Although some question this practice, claiming it will encourage existing employees to recommend anyone for the rewards, this hasn't proven to be the case – staff worry that a poor recommendation will reflect poorly on them. But Analog Devices further discourages it by paying cash only after the new hire has been with the firm for three months.

» **Dangles carrots before candidates**. The Army offers on-the-job training, educational assistance, adventure, and free travel. If you have family, the Army offers support programs, from wellness programs to one-site childcare centers, to spouse employment assistance programs.

» **Provides hiring bonuses**. The Army offers hiring bonuses – and the dollar figure is prominently figured on its Website. The Army has learned how to market off its Website and via CD-ROMs, even customizing the CD-ROMs that can be viewed at the recruitment center. For instance, when the potential recruit clicks on the CD-ROM, he or she is greeted by name, then asked, "Picture yourself in the Army." There are a number of categories, from education to adventure, to money, and based on the sequence of subjects that a prospective candidate chooses, the recruiter has a clearer idea about selling points. Further, the interactive CD-ROM provides a clearer idea to a candidate about what life would actually be like in the Army.

» **Markets from high school on**. The Army starts seeking prospective recruits while they're still in high school. Usually the pitch isn't blatant. Rather, the recruiters offer time to work with problem students or to be substitute teachers. Some high schools even allow the Armed Services to offer elective leadership classes, referred to as the Junior Reserve Officer Training Corps. The idea is to make themselves known so that students will come to them following high school graduation.

Likewise, in college, the Armed Forces offer ROTC programs.

Some companies can emulate this practice by bringing in high school students as interns rather than limit such programs to college students. Even college programs enable young people to become familiar enough with an organization that it's their first choice for an employer – and give the prospective employer an opportunity to decide if the intern is company material.

OPPORTUNISTIC RECRUITMENT

When there wasn't a shortage of people with specific skills in demand, it was possible to wait until the job was open, fill out a requisition specifying the exact requirements the candidate would need, and then go looking for just that person. As the economy goes on a roller coaster ride, it is possible to still do this in some industries and fields. In others, the job market remains tight. It is still tough to match candidates to requirements. Some companies have overcome this problem with opportunistic hiring – that is, by identifying the kind of job a talented candidate would fit and courting that person until one of those jobs becomes available. If need be, they might hire the person. Until the job is available, they might have him or her do special projects and get to know the organization.

There are also organizations that have earmarked jobs as entry points for experienced people – like strategic planning, business development, media staff, and assistant manager. Talent they want are kept in these jobs for a short term until a more suitable job for the candidate is available. Then he or she is moved into that position and the previous job is left vacant for the next incoming hire.

PerkinElmer, a producer of analytical and detection systems, practices opportunistic hiring as part of its recruiting strategy. Actually, it has a headhunter to look for talented people who would make good general managers. Hires take on special projects and learn the business for 12 to 18 months while they wait for the right job to become available. The program lets PerkinElmer hire people with minimal knowledge of their industry.

PerkinElmer hires around four people annually as part of this program. General Electric, which is at least 50 times the size of PerkinElmer, brings more than 100 people a year from consulting firms, accounting companies, the Military, and other fields into its business development, corporate audit positions, and other "transition" assignments. Generally, the people remain from 12 to 18 months in these temporary positions, then move on to more permanent placement. If no position opens up by then, they usually move on. The program began on a corporate level and now has been replicated for each division.

This can be a timely option in today's times, as experienced talent becomes available through downsizings. Rather than wait for an opening, hunt for talent continuously in order to capture people when they are available or ready to make a move.

HIRE THOSE NOT LOOKING

Despite the economy, the market for some disciplines remains tighter than others. IT is a case in point. Electronic Arts (EA), the world's largest video game company, uses its résumé database to keep in touch with game developers who might someday be recruited to the company. The company's Website is used to attract job seekers (EA.com) who are asked questions about career goals and aspirations, backgrounds, interests, and capabilities. The Web script even asks if the company can contact the candidate in the future. Even if the individual is just looking, EA has information on potential hires. Where there are suitable matches, the system notifies EA's hiring matches. In the first year that EA installed the system, it had a pool of 34,000 candidates, of which 20,000 agreed to be contacted.

When the company decided to move its development of its NASCAR game from Silicon Valley to Orlando, Florida, it invited 18,000 of the database's pre-qualified, previously assessed candidates to explore the new opportunities in Orlando. The details of the 40 positions to be filled, required qualifications, and links to apply online were accompanied by a preview of the studio's best graphics and animations and a sneak look at the highly anticipated video game that was being developed in Orlando. Within a month, the company had 3000 candidates who had linked for more information. From there, finding the necessary hires was easy.

DoubleClick uses referrals. Within the first three months of 2000, it was able to find and hire 500 people this way, growing the business by 30%. Employees got $1000 for their first referral, $2000 for their second, and so on, without a ceiling. Altogether, the referral system accounted for 43% of the firm's new hires.

These examples send a message to companies: There are many different ways you might be able to reach candidates in job markets where the pickings are slim.

Once you have good employees, how do you keep them?

SUCCESSFULLY MANAGING PEOPLE

If you consider the practices of companies with low turnover rates, you find that key to high retention is focusing on the people, not on the issue of retention. Steelcase is very much a case in point. It has a turnover rate of 2%, yet it would tell you it doesn't have a retention program *per se*. What it has is a set of core values that demands treatment of employees with dignity and respect against which its supervisors are measured. Every employee also has access to its CEO; any employee can make an appointment to see CEO James Hackett and discuss any issue with him, a practice an average of ten employees monthly take advantage of.

Underlying this open-door policy is a concept that Hackett calls "leverage." As he has explained it, when employees leave at their own discretion, it is usually because they felt they had no control over their work lives. They felt that they couldn't make a difference or that no one would listen to them. His open-door policy, he believes, is one way that the company counters that feeling. Access to the CEO discourages a feeling of powerlessness.

Employees are assured that there will be no retribution by going over their supervisor's head. Indeed, Hackett has promised that any punitive action on a supervisor's part thereafter will lead to the supervisor's termination. On the other hand, all allegations against supervisors are thoroughly investigated. Employees who try to manipulate the open-door system will also be terminated.

Steelcase Inc. is the world's largest manufacturer of office furniture. Based in Grand Rapids, it has operations today in nine countries, including France and Japan. The company was hit hard in the early 1990s when the economy forced it to lay off hourly workers for the first time since its founding in 1912. Fortunately, as the economy turned around, by 1992 it was able to recall all who had been let go and sales returned to earlier days. Six years later the company went public, granting each employee ten shares and an option to purchase 100 more at 15% below the public price.

Still, the downsizing of 1991, 1992, and 1993 continued to be felt. The downsizing had shifted attention from people to profits and consequently morale declined. Initially, the company experimented with the idea that turnover was something good, providing the organization with the opportunity to bring in new ideas with new hires. But as the organization almost went union, it realized it had to begin a healing process. And what better way to do that, management thought, than to recapture the values Steelcase had informally espoused since its inception.

There were six:

1 Act with integrity
2 Tell the truth
3 Keep commitments
4 Treat people with respect
5 Promote positive relationships
6 Promote the environment.

Not only were the values espoused, but the behaviors associated with the values were disseminated to the workforce. A video was even made that declared the company's commitment to these six core values. Hackett attributes this more than anything else to re-energizing the personal contact that was so much a part of the company prior to the layoffs in the early 1990s.

In an effort to do all it can to support the six values, top management periodically distributes an 18-question survey that asks employees to rate how well the managers and executives subscribe to the values – with questions like "To what extent does your manager treat you with respect?" and "To what extent does your supervisor speak the truth?" – and then every manager sits down with his or her direct reports and discusses the results. Based on the survey results, each manager's supervisor is responsible for seeing that an action plan is developed and carried out.

In small groups, the questions have been used to prompt suggestions for how to improve the company's performance in relation to a particular value.

The six core values have also been incorporated into its performance management system for salaried and supervisory personnel. Sixty per cent of ratings is based on the results attained; the other 40% is based on how they got those results. The first six questions about the "how" relate to the values: the extent to which the person treats others with dignity and respect, keeps commitments, tells the truth, etc. A 360-degree assessment is used so evaluators get input from everyone with whom the individual interacts daily.

If an employee has a personal problem – alcohol or drugs, or a family problem – and is fired as a consequence, the company will reconsider his or her return assuming the problem has been resolved. Their return isn't only a matter of humanity, but it makes good business sense. Those who return prove to have much stronger commitment than ever to the company.

When it comes to giving the workforce access to information, it hasn't stopped with Hackett's open-door policy. Steelcase plants hold quarterly business meetings for their managers, in which companywide initiatives are discussed and performance against plant goals is reported. In turn, the managers are charged with sharing the information with the hourly workers. In addition, in each plant, the plant manager and plant financial advisor hold a monthly meeting for all employees during which they present financial data on the company's overall performance and benchmark their plant's performance against the others in the company.

Thus, management believes they have rebuilt the sense of connection with the company that employees lost during the downsizings.

Since turnover can cost between $7500 and $12,000, not counting salary, for the least technical hourly job, the company continues to monitor employee satisfaction. Since lack of opportunity for advancement can demoralize employees, Steelcase provides talented people with numerous opportunities and as much training as they need, much of it paid for, to move up in the company. As important to retention are responsibility and freedom. And at Steelcase, management has made clear to all supervisors that they should allow their direct reports to make more decisions about their work. "We try to maintain an atmosphere where employees are allowed the freedom to do their specific job in their own way," said Ted Wustman, team supervisor, Computer Furniture Plant.

So at Steelcase, retention isn't a package of programs, a bunch of stop-gap retention efforts. Rather, it is corporate culture built around six values, creating a work environment in which the policies and procedures and systems are people-friendly. Which includes:

» opportunities for advancement;
» access to decision-makers;
» fair, uniform standards;
» continuous, work-related (think useful) feedback;
» awards – financial and otherwise – for outstanding performance;
» treatment of employees with dignity and respect; and
» employee empowerment.

All of these factors contribute the kind of people-friendly organization with a low turnover rate.

THE ISSUE OF EMPLOYEE COMMITMENT

The importance of this people-friendly culture is also evident to AlliedSignal. The company had no high turnover rate, but there also wasn't any great employee commitment to the firm, according to Lloyd Wilky, project director for the firm's strategy to drive higher business results through increased employee commitment. The company had undergone major restructuring starting in 1991. By 1993, the results of that full-scale restructuring were evident – more than 15% annual growth and high customer satisfaction rates. But each time the company conducted an employee satisfaction survey, the findings were mediocre – despite efforts in providing learning and career opportunities, good pay and benefits, and the like.

The company's Leadership Committee charged HR with investigating the situation and determining the reasons behind employee dissatisfaction. Needless to say, the cause was the restructuring, which had left employees distrustful of management. Employees also used the term "pressure cooker" to describe the work environment. More work, fewer employees to do it – and no answer to the big WIFM ("What's in it for me?") question from employees.

A variety of initiatives were tried. For instance, the HR group introduced variable pay programs in some areas. But these proved ineffectual. Neither was a cafeteria-style approach to benefits and more options in the 401(k) plan (a group retirement plan).

When these programs didn't work, the company chose to take a broader, "total value" approach to the problem to demonstrate to employees the total value of employment at AlliedSignal. The company decided to offer programs such as medical, dental, 401(k), and the like, but to package them in a manner that better responded to employee needs. This integrated approach was turned down by focus groups of employees who told HR that the improvements management was offering were great but the answer to greater commitment was improved relationship between each employee and his or her supervisor.

The employees were saying exactly what a study at the University of Michigan showed – that is, 70 to 80% of what a person thinks about an organization is directly related to the relationship they have with their boss.

So AlliedSignal modified its initiative to focus on relationships – first, between supervisors and subordinates and, then, the overall relationship between the company and workforce. Toward improving the relationship with supervisors, the company identified five core behaviors that employees said were important for a supervisor to demonstrate. AlliedSignal developed a series of supervisory training programs that were designed to promote the following.

1 **Use of straight talk when communicating.** Employees wanted their supervisors to be open and honest with them.
2 **A willingness to listen.** The employees wanted supervisors to be open to their ideas and suggestions, not only listening to their thoughts but giving them serious consideration. Employees said they wanted to be included in decision-making.
3 **Opportunities to learn.** Employees were required to complete 40 hours of learning a year. But they wanted their supervisors to be actively involved in developing each worker's learning plan and to help with its execution.

4 **Recognition of employees.** The employees said that they expected their supervisors to pay attention to what they did and to acknowledge their accomplishments when they were above and beyond the results expected.

5 **Feedback.** Employees wanted their supervisors to be their coach, providing suggestions for development or improvement. They didn't want to have to wait until their performance appraisal to get feedback from their boss.

Yes, employees liked the idea of flexibility in their benefits package rather than the "one size fits all" approach. So AlliedSignal began to redesign benefits programs to offer more choices in medical and dental plans. Flexible spending accounts were initiated. More investment options were offered in the 401(k) plan, and financial planning assistance was made available to employees.

The company created its Life Events Assistance Program by combining its Employee Assistance Programs and a limited Resource and Referral Service under one provider. Consequently, any US-based employee could call a toll-free number, 24 hours a day, and get assistance with virtually any problem, from child care to elder care, to work/life concerns, to medical problems. Nearly 700 employees take advantage of the program monthly.

AlliedSignal also extended its 40-hour personalized learning plans beyond its exempt employees to its hourly workers. At the company's Learning Center, workers learn the skills they need to reach their current performance goals and to move along their chosen career path. CEO Lawrence Bossidy told *Chief Executive* magazine that he had created the Learning Center because "forever learning has been the road away from darkness. And the more you can keep people in the state of the art, the better they feel about themselves and the better the company is. If we do it better than anybody else, that can be a competitive advantage."

Finally, and critical to increased employee satisfaction, AlliedSignal developed a communication program to let employees know the full extent of benefits and programs available to them. Not only did employees get information on the programs, but also tools that they could use to make these programs more accessible to them. For instance, the "what" of a benefits program was supplemented with "how" information on the ways in which employees could get the most value from the program.

This three-fold initiative has not put an end to the company's efforts to increase employee satisfaction. The company continues to conduct surveys of its employees. After all, as employee needs change, the company has to change accordingly.

KEY INSIGHTS

Market your organization to prospective hires

» Identify interests of high-performers you want to recruit, beyond pay and benefits.
» Alert media about corporate efforts that relate to these interests.
» Mention these activities on your Website.
» Develop brochures that promote the best qualities of your organization, *pro bono* efforts, opportunities for self-development, and growth, and fun.
» Conduct similar marketing campaign internally to keep existing employees.

The Armed Services

» Identify prospective candidates' interests (e.g., career opportunities, job security, adventure, family support).
» Stay in touch with prospective recruits, with updates on programs related to their interests.
» Target recruitment brochures to specific interests of likely recruits.
» Reward for referrals.
» Offer money and other carrots for enlistment.
» Market from high school on.

Opportunistic recruitment

» Incorporate recruitment into the strategic plan.
» Provide short-term assignments until a position becomes available.

» Find positions over the short term to provide broad perspective on the organization.
» Place candidate in a permanent position.

Hire those not looking

» Use the Website to capture résumés.
» Develop a database of prospects' career goals and aspirations, backgrounds, interests, and capabilities.
» Screen prospects against vacancy database to identify suitable candidates.
» Follow up with traditional interview.

Successfully managing people

» Build employee retention on a positive work culture/climate.
» Act with integrity.
» Tell the truth.
» Keep commitments.
» Treat people with respect.
» Promote positive relationships.
» Promote the environment.
» Focus on relationships.
» Use straight talk when communicating.
» Demonstrate a willingness to listen.
» Give employees an opportunity to learn.
» Offer recognition.
» Train supervisors to be fair and supportive.

Key Concepts and Thinkers

The glossary associated with recruitment and retention has grown as companies have explored new techniques to seek out qualified managers and employees and reduce turnover. This chapter shares the A to Z of recruitment and retention, including the use of the following in relation to recruitment and retention:

» videotaping
» simulations
» online search
» résumé screening
» retention plan.

Active listening – This entails listening to not only what is said but what isn't said, to putting aside personal feelings to listen objectively to what is said, rephrasing to ensure understanding, and staying focused on what is being said.

Applicant (a.k.a. candidate) – This is a prospective hire, usually someone who has moved beyond pre-screening and has been invited to come in for an interview.

Background – A factor used in matching job candidates to positions, it includes education and job history of prospects, often used as a category in résumés.

Blind ads – These are employment ads in which the name of the employer is not listed. Applicants usually reply to a box number.

Boyatzis, Richard – Before the use of competencies, skills, abilities, and knowledge, as determined by researching how successful employees and managers performed selection and recruitment, were based on job analysis and job requirements as specified in the job description. To this day, that is still often the case. However, the work by Boyatzis, as described in his book *The Competent Manager: A Model for Effective Performance*, has led to increased use of competencies, carefully identified via interviews with and comparisons of work performance between best and mediocre performers in the same or similar jobs. Boyatzis' work was designed not only to improve recruitment but also job performance, which is its usual practice in the US. In the UK, however, the focus is very different which may also explain the difference in terminology. In the UK, the word is "competence," not "competency," and the focus is on job standardization. The National Council for Vocational Qualifications focuses on defining the tasks and outcomes required of the job, then uses this information to set standards or expected outcomes.

Brain drain – This phrase reflects departure of talented employees due to better job opportunities elsewhere or corporate activities (like downsizing) and prompt migration elsewhere by employees.

Career pathing – Employees are assessed to determine their potential and what steps they must take to move up into positions that fit their career plans and corporate needs.

Closed question – This question, in the context of job interviews, is designed to find out specific facts or gain commitment or confirmation on an issue. They often start with the word "can," "did," "would," or "will." Sample: "Can you use Word 2000?"

Chronological résumé – These are résumés that organize job listings by dates of employment.

Classified ads – These are ads placed in a special section of the paper that contains the help wanted ads.

Closed shop – A closed shop is a company that hires only members of the union with which it has a contract. See also Union shop.

College recruiters – Also called campus recruiters, these are specialized members of an HR department whose major task is to contact and visit colleges all over a nation to seek graduates to fill their companies' need for college-trained people.

Competency model – Based on work by Richard Boyatzis, the competency model uses skills, abilities, knowledge, and attitudes to determine best qualified candidates rather than rely solely on past job experience. The 12 most common competencies, according to Robert Wood and Tim Payne, authors of *Competency-Based Recruitment and Selection: A Practical Guide*, are communication, results/achievement, customer focus, teamwork, leadership, planning and organizing, business awareness, flexibility/adaptability, developing others, problem solving, analytical thinking, and building relationships.

Contingent workforce – The contingent workforce is made up of a variety of workers who are not formally on staff. In the beginning, the term referred primarily to clerical support, but now includes almost every job title, from employee to CEO. These individuals "solo" professionally.

Development plan – Post-hiring, supervisors should create a development plan for new hires in order to fill any skill voids. The plan can entail formal training or use of a body to familiarize the new hire with company procedures.

Dikel, Margaret – An expert in recruitment issues, she is creator of *The Riley Guide*, an Internet directory that identifies the best sites for online recruitment.

Disposable employees – A term coined by Martha R.A. Fields, an HR authority, in her book *Indispensable Employees*. The term reflected hundreds of thousands of employees laid off in the late 1980s and early 1990s.

Empathetic listener – One who listens with his or her heart as well as his or her head. Empathetic listeners put themselves in the shoes of those who are speaking, trying to feel what the other person is feeling.

Employer of choice – The title given to organizations based on low turnover due to a strategic and tactical approach to employee retention, including creation of a supportive culture and fair application of policies and procedures.

Employment agency counselor – Staff members at recruitment firms who take job orders, interview applicants, and make referrals.

Employment at will – This is a legal concept under which an employee is hired and can be fired at the will of the employer. Unless restricted by law or contract, the employer has the right to refuse to hire an applicant or to terminate an employee for any reason or no reason at all.

Executive recruiters – These are consultants who specialize in recruiting and screening senior executives and other top-level personnel. Often called headhunters.

Exit interview – A meeting is held with the departing occupant of the job to gain a good understanding of what the job entails and the problems involved, how the job relates to the organization and other employees. If the job has changed since it was last filled, then the exit interview should determine why. Information from the exit interview may also reveal why the previous occupant chose to leave, information that can be incorporated into retention efforts. Also called separation interview.

Expats – These are nationals who work abroad.

Functional résumé – This is a résumé that presents an applicant's background by listing duties, responsibilities, or accomplishments without regard to the job or company in which they were performed.

H-1B workers – government classification for workers from overseas.

Halo effect – This is said to occur when a recruiter, because of one or two outstanding characteristics, assumes the candidate is outstanding in all other critical factors.

Headhunters – See Executive recruiters.

Herzberg, Frederick – Herzberg's motivational research in the 1950s and 1960s identified those factors that make the difference between job satisfaction and dissatisfaction and thereby have an impact on job retention. Herzberg called those factors that influence satisfaction "hygiene factors." They include a good relationship with manager or supervisor, interpersonal relationships, physical working conditions, salary, company policies and administrative practices, benefits, and job security. Interestingly, it is not their existence, but their lack of existence that has an impact on motivation and on contentment with a work environment. Later work by Herzberg coined the term "job enrichment" and suggested how organizations could generate employee enthusiasm by providing more opportunity for them to use their creativity. If you look at "employers of choice," you see evidence of job enrichment career management, self-development, self-managed learning, even empowerment. Gary Hamel said, "Pay for performance, employee stock ownership plans, end-of-year bonuses – too many organizations seem to believe that the only motivation to work is an economic one. Teaching knowledge assets like Skinnerian rats is hardly the way to get the best out of people. Herzberg offered a substantially more subtle approach – one that still has much to recommend it."

Hypothetical questions – These questions test an applicant's reaction in specific situations. They address situations that might happen to the candidate should he or she get the job. Sample: "If you had to deal with an aggressive customer, what would you do?"

Impats – These are foreign nationals who are imported to work in another company.

Internet referral services – The equivalent of the classified ad section of newspapers, these Websites post job listings, applicants list their résumés, and matches are made by employers and prospective employees. Example: www.monster.com.

Interview – This is a meeting between the interviewer and the candidate to determine match between applicant and company.

Investigative agencies – There are firms that check on applicants' reputation in the community, criminal records, and employment history prior to a hiring decision being made.

Job analysis – This is a study of a job to identify the responsibilities that fall within the job and skills and background required to do the job effectively.

Job bank – This is a database listing all the skills, education, experience, and other background of employees. Within companies, this database can be searched to match job openings against the current workforce to hire from within. Also called skill banks.

Job description – The job description is a document that includes the job title, key responsibilities, level of authority of the position and reporting relationship of the job holder to others within the organization, grade or position within a compensation or other pecking order, and qualifications. It is developed by the human resources manager or person to whom the job holder reports, or both, and helps in preparing want ads and assessing candidates.

Job specifications – These are the qualifications a person needs to be considered for the job opening.

Leading questions – In the context of job interviews, they are poorly phrased questions that generate the response desired by the interviewer. Sample: "I suppose in your past job you have had to be very organized."

Maslow, Abraham – This behavioral scientist is best known for his "hierarchy of needs," a concept he first published in 1943. Maslow argued that there was an ascending order of needs that had to be understood for people to be motivated. First, there are the physiological needs of warmth, shelter, and food. Once these basic needs are met, others emerge to dominate. Next come the safety needs, then social or love needs, and then ego or self-esteem needs. Ultimately, with each need satisfied comes what Maslow labeled "self-actualization," as the individual achieves his or her own personal potential. As downsizings increase, we may see lower needs of greater concern to employees in particular, issues of safety and security which can lead to continued turnover despite a tight job market.

Negligent hiring – Because of failure to check references, ensure skills, or otherwise check an applicant's ability, the wrong candidate is hired. Often, the term is used in legal situations in which a wrong hiring decision is behind a costly business mistake, accident that hurts a co-worker or customer, or violation of the law (e.g., hire of bus driver with history of traffic accidents or bank clerk with credit problems).

Nondirective interviewing - Instead of making a substantive remark after an applicant's response, the interviewer makes a comment such as "uh-huh" or just nods her head or remains silent, thereby encouraging the candidate to continue talking. The goal is to bring out more information.

Online recruitment - Use of broad-based and niched recruitment sites to acquire résumés to fill job vacancies.

Open questions - These are questions, in this context asked of applicants, that demand more than a "yes" or "no" reply. Their intention is to get the candidate to talk openly about a topic and established facts. Usually "how" and "why" questions, less frequently "what," "where," and "who" questions, they are designed to extract as much information as possible about the candidate's skills, qualities, attributes, aptitudes, and abilities. Sample: "How would you deal with a difficult customer?"

Orientation program - These are programs designed to give new hires a better start on the job by familiarizing them with job rules and operating procedures. Ideally, these sessions should also include a discussion of the department's mission and that mission's relationship to the corporate strategy.

Panel interviews - Rather than a candidate being interviewed by a single person, a panel interview has the applicant sit down with several interviewers and collectively they conduct the interview.

Perks - Short for perquisites, these are goods or services given to an employee in addition to regular salary and benefits as an incentive to attract and keep hires.

Pitchfork effect - The opposite of the halo effect, this attitude occurs when one poor characteristic of a job candidate darkens all subsequent discussion of his or her background.

Prescreening - This aspect of the screening process precedes inviting an applicant for an interview.

Probing questions - In the context of job interviews, probing questions test the depth of a candidate's knowledge or experience, or simply the honesty of a reply, seeking out further facts to support the candidate's remark.

Qualifications - These are the skills, abilities, knowledge, and experiences necessary for the job holder to perform the job satisfactorily.

Some job specifications divide qualifications under two headings: essential and desirable.

Recruitment process – This is the means by which a vacancy is filled. The same procedure is usually used to fill new jobs as well as to find a replacement for an existing vacant job.

Retention strategies – These are strategies designed to keep talented employees with their employer. They may involve compensation packages, perks, involvement in high-visibility activities, or access to extra training to increase employability.

Separation interview – See Exit interview.

Simulations – A technique during interviews to measure the capability of candidates. The nature of simulations reflect the job opening, from demonstration of skills to management tasks like leadership of a team meeting or coaching session for an HR/trainer prospect.

Soloing – The act of working on one's one (e.g., freelance).

Structured interview – See WASP structure.

Talent war – This is a phrase that has become popular to describe the competition for skilled workers.

Temps – These are people who do work for the company, but are not employed by the firm. They are on the payroll of the company as temps or on the payroll of a temporary-staffing or employee-leasing service. Usually they are used for short-term assignments, for instance, filling in for an absent employee or augmenting staffing needs due to seasonal work levels.

Turnover – This refers to the numbers of employees who leave a company to be replaced by other workers.

Union shop – A company is a union shop if it can hire nonunion members, but they must join the union tied to the company within a specified time after being hired.

WASP structure – This refers to the four phases of a well-run interview: W for "welcome" or greeting; A for "asking questions," to gauge the applicant's suitability for the job; S for "supply," which refers to the interviewer's responsibility to answer questions of the applicant; and P for "part company" or end the interview, during which the interviewer thanks the applicant for coming and describes the next stage of the hiring process. Also called Structured interview.

Videoconferencing - Used in the context of recruitment, an increasing means to interview candidates located in other cities or countries, thereby allowing companies to expand the reach of their recruitment process beyond local companies.

Weddle, Peter D. - Publisher of *Weddle's: The Newsletter for Successful Online Recruitment*, Weddle is regarded as an authority on most effective use of the Internet/Websites for recruitment.

Resources

There has been much written about recruitment and retention. This chapter identifies some of the many resources available:

» books
» articles
» surveys
» Websites.

ARTICLES

Fyock, C.D. (1999) "101 ideas for getting the employees you want." The Workforce Stability Institute, www.employee.org/article_101_ideas_getting_what_you_want.html. Here is a to-do list for HR professionals to maximize the effectiveness of time spent on recruitment. The list includes some basics in recruitment – like use of government-funded employment and training programs and community groups that provide access to older workers, moms interested in returning to work, and the disabled – but it also includes marketing tips, like how direct mail campaigns can help with tough-to-fill jobs, and the worth of free career planning workshops, posters and signs with tear-off application forms in local businesses, and telemarketing campaigns to provide access to new prospects.

Hacker, C.A. (October 1997) "The cost of poor hiring decisions ... and how to avoid them." *HRFocus*. Companies incur unnecessary added costs from poor employee recruitment. One study by the US Department of Labor found bad hiring decisions can cost a business as much as a new hire's first year's earnings. These costs stem from such factors as advertising, training a replacement, potential customer loss, decreased productivity, low employee morale, and a possible unemployment compensation claim. Why are the wrong people hired? Recruiters often talk too much and listen too little. Since the wrong hire can lower department morale, the author goes beyond the issue of recruitment to a manager's role as coach or counselor should the wrong hiring decision be made. Failure to act as soon as the mistake is discovered can add to direct costs.

Zingheim, P.K. and Schuster, J.R. (2001) "Total rewards and the better workforce deal." *MWorld* (www.mworld.org). What are total rewards? It is a four-part formula: It is (1) a compelling future; (2) individual growth – opportunity for training; (3) a positive work climate and culture; and (4) total rewards, which includes base pay, cash incentives, stock options, and recognition. The old deal, say the authors, rewarded tenure rather than performance and skill growth. Workers owned their jobs. As we moved into the 1990s, we experienced downsizing, reengineering, rightsizing, and flattening. Companies expected people to meet more than halfway to acquire and apply the skills the company needed to succeed. During the economic boom of the late 1990s, we experienced a better workforce deal. People don't want to be seen as commodities. This deal supported mutual choice by companies and workforces – more coaching, developmental feedback, training, and nurturing that result in better understanding, acceptance of goals, and improved business outcomes. We're talking about a positive workplace with a compelling future that invests in the people and also provides attractive rewards.

Raphael, T. (September 2001) "Hold the line on salaries and benefits." *Workforce*. HR is in a squeeze. There's pressure to raise or maintain salaries to stay competitive. But there is even greater pressure to cut costs across the board – beginning with pay cuts, then moving on to downsizing, depending on the financial vulnerability of the business. Those companies that either haven't found downsizing to be enough or want to avoid downsizing are turning to across-the-board pay cuts, cuts in health benefits or their contribution to premiums, and forced unpaid vacations, sabbaticals, and days off. What are the implications to recruitment and retention? The labor shortage hasn't evaporated – anything under 5% of unemployment means that recruiters still have to scrape to get talent – and there are still tough-to-fill positions. So cuts in 401(k) plans is unwise. Companies are looking to benefits like tuition refund for hard-to-fill jobs and refund for certification for those jobs demanding it. Money is a major recruitment device but HR managers may have to promote nonfinancial rewards in a balancing act in which recruitment and retention of the best is on one side and keeping payroll acceptable to senior management is on the other side.

BOOKS

Levering, R. and Moskowitz, M. (1994, with periodic updates). *The 100 Best Companies to Work for in America*. Plume, New York, NY. Primarily for job seekers, this book is still an excellent resource for HR professionals who want to stay current on what the most progressive companies are doing to attract and retain excellent employees. Using a scale of one to five stars, the authors rate companies in the following six areas: pay and benefits, opportunities, job security, pride in work and company, openness and fairness, and camaraderie and friendliness. Each of the employers of choice get three to four pages of description, and there are interviews throughout with HR managers at these "best" companies.

Fitz-Enz, J. (1997). *The 8 Practices of Exceptional Companies*. AMACOM, New York, NY. This author's focus on "best practices" is on the human asset – the people whose work is the basis of an organization's success. Jac Fitz-Enz, who is founder and president of the Saratoga Institute, Santa Clara, CA, devoted four years in a study of 1000 companies and isolated eight people-related practices that, he says, improve productivity. In describing these – from two-way communication to a relationship between culture and operation – he also describes innovative staffing approaches like First Tennessee Bank with its internal "talent pool" of applicants who have agreed to take part-time jobs until full-time positions become available.

Hacker, C.A. (1997). *The High Cost of Low Morale*. Saint Lucie Press. As the author demonstrates, low morale translates into high turnover. A training consultant, Carol Hacker has worked with HR departments in both large and small companies, and she has found that practices designed to enhance employee morale and motivation significantly impact the bottom line. The book itself consists of 100 or more three-or-four-paragraph "lessons" in effective people management, including hiring, orientation, and employee retention.

Nelson, R. (1994) *101 Ways to Reward Employees*. Thomas Allen Ltd, New York, NY. The book cover suggests that "money isn't every-thing." But it can be very important. In today's economic downturn, it isn't as available as it was during the boom years. Consequently, the low-cost, proven strategies that management specialist Bob Nelson suggests may be more valuable today than perhaps two or three years ago. Still, in boom and bust, this book has been a best seller for both managers and HR professionals with its case studies of company-wide programs and quick tips that seem so simple yet can sustain motivation, like Chevron's Treasure Chest, with gifts that supervisors can use to reward employees on the spot for outstanding performance, or Home Depot's merit badge and plaque on which all recipients of a badge have their name, and the "scratch off" cards with various awards that are given to employees at Busch Gardens, Tampa, FL who have offered exceptional service to guests.

Rosse, J. and Levin, R. (2001). *Talent Flow: A Strategic Approach to Keeping Good Employees, Helping Them Grow, and Letting Them Go*. Jossey-Bass, San Francisco, CA. By its title, this book would seem to focus solely on management retention. Not so. Rather, it describes a strategic approach to employee management that addresses the flow of people into and through an organization and their performance while they are employed. It's as valuable during a downturn as an uptrend in the economy because it begins with a fundamental belief: People will inevitably leave your organization. The authors observe that there are various reasons, including one relevant to this book: Hiring errors occur in every organization. Where the problem leads to a mismatch, it can contribute to a third belief of the authors: Some good performers inevitably become poor performers. The authors suggest that quitting may be one of the most benign responses a dissatisfied employee can make – infectious mediocre performance is much more serious. This book suggests retention strategies tied to recruitment and performance, appropriate strategies to address performance issues, even information for planning and implementing layoffs and reductions in workforce when they become necessary.

Michaels, E., Handfield-Jones, H. and Axelrod, B. (2001). *The War for Talent*. Harvard Business School Press, Cambridge, MA. The ideas for this book are based on results of the McKinsey & Company survey conducted by the same three authors in 1997 and again in 2000. While the authors did their original research at the height of the economic boom, they argue that the war for talent continues. Although it is being waged on various fronts, their book focuses on the ''intensifying demand for high-caliber managerial talent.'' They point to the findings in 2000 in which 99% of the corporate officers in their survey said their managerial talent pool needs to be much stronger three years from then. Only 20% said they had sufficient talent to pursue most of their companies' business opportunities. They believe that smaller companies and startups will continue to absorb a fair amount of talent – regardless of the dot-com crash – so mid- and larger-sized companies will need to craft a winning employee value proposition. With funds short and stock options of limited interest given the rocky market, the authors suggest the value of other benefits, like increased employability. As they observe, talent rarely arrives fully developed. Opportunities to refine managerial competencies and projects in which to demonstrate capability may address financial shortfalls.

Wood, R. and Payne, T. (1998). *Competency-Based Recruitment and Selection: A Practical Guide*. Wiley & Sons Ltd, New York, NY. This book points out how a knowledge of the competencies required in a job can facilitate a closer match between a candidate's skills and interests and the demands of the job for which he is applying. The authors show how competencies can be the underpin for a full range of recruitment and retention strategies – from application forms and interviews to subsequent orientation and motivation to sustain job satisfaction.

Branham, L. (2001). *Keeping the People Who Keep You in Business*. AMACOM, New York, NY. An employee-retention expert, Leigh Branham provides HR professionals and their organizations with a plan to retain employees, via 24 compelling strategies. The strategies are grouped under four key thoughts: (1) Be a company that people want to work for – an employer of choice; (2) select the right people in the first place; (3) get them off to a good start; and (4) coach and reward to sustain commitment. The book itself contains numerous examples, like "Hire and promote managers who have the talent to manage people," an Eaton Corporation program that bases 20% of each manager's bonus opportunity on how well the manager maintains low turnover or reduces high turnover. The cases are of interest, but the foundation on which all are based may be more important in today's uncertain times since, with the exception of the first, money need not be a deciding factor in achievement.

SURVEYS

Kepner-Tregoe, Princeton, NJ (1999). *Avoiding the Brain Drain: What Companies Are Doing to Lock in Their Talent*. Kepner-Tregoe surveyed 1290 employees – 541 managers and 749 hourly workers – on employee turnover. That they felt that employee turnover, especially among the best and brightest, being a growing problem was not news. Nor was it news that in lean organizations the loss of even a few high-performing employees can have a significant effect on business success. Less expected was the fact that responses suggested that money, while a motivator, wasn't as important as thought. Both managers and workers pointed to feeling valued, knowing there is room for advancement, and having a conflict-free relationship with their supervisor as critical factors in the retention equation. The researchers went further and investigated the practices of 11 "employers of choice," companies identified via *Fortune's "100 Best Companies to Work for in America."* The study of companies like Corning and Johnson & Johnson confirmed the initial research – the 11 companies went beyond individual programs to creation of a positive work culture and climate, with attention on the role of the supervisor in sustaining worker satisfaction.

HayGroup, Inc., New York, NY (2001). *The Retention Dilemma: Why Productive Workers Leave – Seven Suggestions for Keeping Them.* Done as the economy shifted from boom to bust, this survey showed that an economic downturn will not prevent a mobile employee – top talent – from moving on, with serious consequences for his or her former employer. The survey by HayGroup found the gap between committed and exiting workers were tied to their skills not having been tapped and their lack of confidence in the company's management and direction. These were followed by the abundance of opportunities for advancement, the chance to learn new skills, and the availability of coaching and counseling from supervisors.

THE WEB

Recruitment sites

Career Builder Network (www.careerbuilder.com). There is no résumé database on this site, but the job board allows posting of listings on more than 25 major career sites including USA Today, NBC, and others. The cost for a listing is a little over $100.

CareerPath (www.careerpath.com). This Website combines listings from various employers' Websites as well as help wanted listings from newspapers across the US. The cost to post an ad is $200/month and $3000/year to search the database. No listing remains on the site for more than two weeks.

Headhunter.net (www.headhunter.net). Linked, among other sites, to jobsearch.com, Headhunter.net is popular to recruiters since its posting fee remains under $100. The site's best feature may be its geographical search capabilities that allow it to recognize over 250,000 locales worldwide. The cost to use the 160,000 entry database ranges from $0 to $1500 yearly.

HotJobs.com (www.hotjobs.com). This database has in excess of 300,000 résumés and the costs are $150 to post ads and $500 to search résumés. With screening tools built in to the job search categories for prospective employees, it makes this site popular for US-based recruiters.

JobOptions (www.joboptions.com). A Website for all fields and categories, the prime attraction of this site is the ease of submitting job postings (via e-mail) and the opportunity to describe at length job openings. Employers can even post their own ads and links on the site. Costs are $395 to place an ad and $2250/year to access the database of over 227,000.

Jobs.com (www.jobs.com). This site focuses on major cities and geographical areas across the US. Employers can seek out employees close to their operations, as well. Jobs.com offers software that can help sort résumés as well as track the hiring process. Résumés are updated and new postings appear daily. There is no résumé older than three months on the site, which boasts 1.5 million résumés. Cost to post a job listing is $99/month.

Monster.com (www.monster.com). One of the biggest job boards on the Web, it offers employers a large slate of useful features such as résumé routing, quick résumé database searches, screening tools, the opportunity to publish one's company profile, and high name recognition among visitors. The focus is primarily on tech jobs. The résumé database size is estimated at one million, and the cost to post an employment ad is under $300. You can lease the opportunity to search the Monster.com résumé database for $2000 (for a three-month window).

Web information sites

HIREadigm. For employees seeking jobs, headhunters.net has a newsletter entitled CareerBytes (http://www.headhunter.net/JobSeeker/CareerBytes/Index.htm). For employers, headhunters.net offers a newsletter, *HIREadigm* (http://www.headhunter.net/JobPoster/

Hireadigm/Index.htm), that offers HR managers advice on how to identify and hire the best candidates. A monthly onsite newsletter, *HIREadigm* offers how-to information on traditional and not-so-traditional (e.g., teleconferencing) recruitment techniques. You don't have to read the current contents or access its archive.

HR.com. This Canada-based Website doesn't cover solely staffing issues. There are sections as well on labor relations, HRIS, and compensation and benefits, to name just a few other categories. You'll have to register, but once you do you can access the new and past articles on any of the subjects and any section on the site. There is also information on firms that can assist you, tools you can use off the site and other tools you can purchase to help you, and even coverage of a variety of HR events.

WORKFORCE. It's a Website (http://workforce.com/), but it is also a monthly magazine that registering on the site gets you for free. On the Website, you can check out the most recent issue or access the archive even without registering. On both, you will find free articles on compensation, benefits, and rewards; legal issues; recruitment and retention; software and technology; and training and development. Besides articles, you will find tips and tools and product case studies. The 96-page, four-color magazine covers trends and developments of interest not only to HR professionals but managers concerned with people management issues.

IOMA.com Management Library. You have to register to get access to articles from this print publisher. There is also a fee to read and print content from the archive, which includes content from its print newsletters *HRFocus* and *Human Resources Department Management Report*. Once you have registered on the site, you can also register for one of its free e-newsletters – from *HR News and Views* and *Personnel Policy* to *Leadership Newswire* and *Business Technology*. Single articles from the archive cost from $4 to $6 each; an entire issue can be accessed for $25.

The Workforce Stability Institute (www.employee.org) is a non-profit research and education organization that offers consulting services, training programs, and articles on employee retention strategies of companies of all sizes.

Ten Steps to Making Recruitment and Retention Work

Being successful at recruitment and retention means:

» plan ahead;
» define the job before you start;
» identify multiple sources for recruitment;
» prescreen candidates;
» ask the right questions;
» match candidates to requirements;
» make a good first impression;
» provide challenging work;
» don't overlook compensation and pay and working conditions; and
» train managers to ensure fair supervision.

Attention focused on recruitment and retention during the economic boom. The worldwide economic downturn, due to financial and political reasons, shouldn't cause you to stop paying attention to these issues. These tough economic times may be perfect to assess your organization's existing talent and ensure that those you hire are the very best available and, equally important, the top talent you hire or who are currently on staff – those who can help drive performance when it is so critical to your organization's survival – remain.

Here are 10 critical steps to successful recruitment and retention. As you read, keep in mind that there is actually an 11th factor in today's topsy-turvy economy: employer loyalty. The downsizing of the early 1990s led to much of the job-hopping by employees during good times. They figured that employers showed little concern for them, so why should they care about the impact of their departure on their employer. A demonstration of loyalty to your current employees can prevent the loss of your more mobile employees during the tough times and their continued desire to stay with you when the opportunities to jump ship for a better vessel return.

1. PLAN AHEAD

Although we may know that someone in the organization will likely leave, too often we wait to seek a replacement until that individual quits or is fired. Likewise, if we have plans in place that will demand additional staffing, we may wait until the very last minute to begin the search for a suitable candidate. Both can create workflow problems. Rather than delay, we should initiate the search as soon as one seems needed. After all, it can take several weeks and sometimes months to find some hires.

While the ideal candidate rarely exists, preplanning can help us identify candidate requirements that will make it easier to fill the position. We should consider not only those who are looking for positions, but those who are employed but fit our needs well, and could be courted to make a job move. Now, before the actual need arises, may be the time to begin the courtship, to determine what could be the basis for interest in a job change.

2. DEFINE THE JOB BEFORE YOU START

Is the job new or are you filling an existing one? In either case, before you start the recruitment process, you need to know exactly what standards you are going to use to measure your candidates. The clearer your thinking, the easier and less arbitrary your selection process.

If the job is new, you are in the position to design the ideal candidate. Draft a job description that fully describes all the tasks and responsibilities of the position and the minimum necessary requirements and experience.

What if you are filling an existing position? Take a look at the job description of the previous occupant of the position to determine if changes are needed. Needs change, and the job may either have changed during the time in which the previous occupant held it, or the needs of the organization for someone in the job may now differ. This, again, is your opportunity to write a job description that reflects exactly the tasks and requirements of the position.

3. IDENTIFY MULTIPLE SOURCES FOR RECRUITMENT

Keep in mind that you may have few openings to fill during difficult economic times. But even in better economic circumstances, it is smart to use as many sources as possible to find the very best talent you can acquire for your firm. You may have found an excellent candidate on one occasion through a headhunter or an employment agency, but don't depend on one or the other the next time to find that individual you want.

Open your mind to other options – in particular, to instituting a program of referrals within your organization in which employees are even financially rewarded for finding successful job/candidate matches. Such matches have been found often to be the most successful – perhaps due to the fact that those who recommend these candidates realize that their own reputation will be influenced by the referral's success or failure.

Experience has shown that the most effective referral programs aren't based solely on bounty payments to employees who bring successful new employees on board. Rather, they are programs well designed, with clear directions about the process for submitting résumés and criteria for award payouts; creation of brochures that outline the program, including instructions for résumé submissions, and regular reminders at company gatherings and through the intranet; a clear understanding that the referring employee's task is solely to encourage a potential hire to consider your organization – the decision as to the suitability of the candidate is best made by those experienced in recruitment, like those in HR; a firm commitment from senior management for the duration of the referral program, since such programs may take three or four hires before they develop the momentum you want; and finally, specific standards for referral submissions, not to disqualify any legitimate leads, but to ensure that there are no conflicts among employees regarding who made the referral first and deserves the reward.

Don't neglect, either, other nontraditional ways to locate talent, like participation in job fairs within the community or on college campuses, which is particularly effective in locating candidates for entry-level positions. Certainly, investigate how to leverage your Website to find job candidates, too. And, of course, list any openings you may have with one or more of the online recruitment sites specific to your industry's needs. It will enable you to broaden your recruiting reach, and it's relatively cheap – the average cost to post a job on an Internet job board is much less expensive than newspaper advertising. Most job boards are free, with the average cost around $200, compared to $15,000 to $20,000 via a search firm.

One of the more novel approaches is to undertake a direct mail marketing campaign. If you use snail mail, this can cost not only the list of potential names, but also postage. A list of e-mail addresses can make the process less costly. And it can be an effective way to locate suitable candidates for a hard-to-fill position.

4. PRESCREEN CANDIDATES

Whether a candidate responded to an ad or was referred by another source you use, the interview with the individual will take time – to eliminate the unqualified and to identify those worthy of further consideration. Depending on the nature and level of a job position, the job interview can take anywhere from 10 minutes to an hour for each prospective candidate. This can be time-intensive if you are a department head or a senior executive and your day is already full with other tasks or you are a human resources manager and interviewing is how you spend much of your workday.

Consequently, you want to reduce the number of individuals you will interview to your most likely prospects. This means prescreening applicants – which means developing the ability to separate the facts from the fluff in job résumés. There are numerous writing tricks that candidates will use, from re-titling previous jobs to make them seem more suitable for the position, to not listing dates of employment but rather number of years in each position to muddy a downward career path, to describing the functions of past jobs rather than the applicants' responsibilities in each job, which may be very different.

Other traps to beware of: gaps in dates; more space given to earlier jobs than to more recent ones; and overemphasis on education and non-job-related experience.

The most effective résumés are those that play up job *tasks* less and play up *accomplishments* in each job more. What makes the applicant stand out in competition with others who have similar experience? Many applicants will use their job descriptions to describe their past work, which is fine so long as they add some of the specific results achieved doing the job. Even then, however, recruiters need to be prepared to ask very pointed questions during the subsequent interviews to ensure that the facts as written are true.

5. ASK THE RIGHT QUESTIONS

Although there are numerous books and courses on how to conduct job interviews, a high percentage of interviews are badly constructed and poorly conducted, and consequently fail to accomplish their objective – which is to identify that one person most suited to fill the position.

The interview is neither a polite conversation nor an interrogation, although the key to the most successful interviews is in the questions asked – and the follow-up questions after the applicant's answer. Rather than move from one question on your list to another, listen to each response, then probe further for more information. Do this throughout each interview to get as much information as possible about applicants.

An answer to one question can open the door to many more questions that can provide insights into a prospect's qualifications before moving on to the next question on the list.

Needless to say, questions should be related to the work involved in the job. So, questions drafted prior to the interview should reflect the requirements as specified in the job description. Review the résumés of each candidate as well, noting any specific areas you need to explore with the individual based on the job in mind. If you have doubts about an applicant, this is the time to address them by asking for specifics about accomplishments claimed.

Throughout, take notes. Don't rely on your memory.

6. MAKE THE RIGHT SELECTION BY MATCHING CANDIDATE TO REQUIREMENTS

That's the intent in the recruitment process. It can be very tempting to select someone "almost right" in order to fill the vacancy, but this can be a serious mistake. It is equivalent to trying to make a square piece of wood fit into a round hole. It is better to continue to search until a proper fit is found.

While you should consider how well the candidate's background fits the requirements, consider, also, the intangibles – factors like an applicant's ability to work in a team, communicate ideas, work under pressure, be flexible, and the like.

Recruiters say that the best selections are those made based on more than one or two factors. And definitely not by one or two of the least important factors. A big selection mistake is choosing a candidate who qualifies in several of the requirements but is weak in the essential responsibilities. There are certain aspects of most jobs in which experience or technical know-how is essential and cannot be taught overnight. Any candidate chosen should satisfy these requirements at a minimum.

7. MAKE A GOOD FIRST IMPRESSION

During the boom days, employers complained about new hires who stayed for only a few months, then moved on to a higher-paying job. In today's economy, that is less likely. Still, it is important during the first few days on the job that new employees get to feel that they are part of the group to minimize any initial dissatisfaction with the job change.

Supervisors can play an important part in this, acquainting new hires to the mission and background of the team. Tell him or her about past projects and challenging assignments. Depending on the work involved, you might want to choose one of the members of the current group to mentor the new hire. He or she can take a special interest in the newcomer, showing him or her "the ropes," which includes answering questions about the work, the company culture, and other staffers, and in general helping the new member get started.

8. PROVIDE CHALLENGING WORK

Research shows that individuals who successfully accomplish mentally challenging work are more satisfied and happy with their jobs. They are less likely to seek work elsewhere if their present assignments "test their mettle."

So if you want to retain your very best employees, it is imperative that your organization ensure that your employees, especially your most talented, feel challenged in their work situations. That demands that you spend sufficient time with each of these individuals to determine what aspects of their jobs are most motivational. Provide coaching to enable them to reach new heights of success. It is important to offer demanding and challenging assignments, but you also need to give them the training and resources to achieve the results you ask for. Certainly don't pigeonhole your very best people. If you can't offer promotion, offer opportunities for increased responsibility. You don't want your very best people doing repetitive, dull tasks, so organize tasks to make the most of the work opportunities.

9. DON'T FORGET ABOUT COMPENSATION AND PAY AND WORKING CONDITIONS

Yes, employees will stay and be happier in organizations where they are able to work on jobs or projects that they find personally interesting. On the other hand, they also expect to be compensated fairly and equitably with others in their job, profession, and industry.

There are intrinsic and extrinsic reasons why people leave a job. Compensation is the most frequently mentioned extrinsic factor. Not only do employees want their pay to be comparable to that of counterparts in other organizations, but they also want to be rewarded for outstanding efforts. Which explains their desire to stay abreast of how the organization is doing.

So pay is one factor. But so is working conditions. A study by the American Society of Interior Designers found that the most important attributes people want in a physical work space are (in order of importance): cleanliness; visual appeal; well-lit and bright, new furniture and equipment; access to people and equipment; quiet and privacy; comfortable furniture; good air quality; nice windows; and a view.

This all doesn't mean that you have to spend lavishly on improving the office or plant. But it does mean you have to be sensitive to inadvertently creating counterproductive work environments from being too tight-fisted. If money is short, at least ask staff for input on workspace design and layout to satisfy their intrinsic need for a voice in the final workspace.

10. TRAIN MANAGERS TO ENSURE FAIR SUPERVISION

There is much talk today about the need for job satisfaction. As you probe to determine what that means to employees, often it is the same: the opportunity to work for managers they can trust and respect. If you want long-term relationships with your best and brightest employees, then you need to ensure they are well and fairly supervised.

Employees want their supervisors to be clear, open, and honest with them. They appreciate a manager who gets everything out on the table, then listens to their viewpoint. They want the opportunity to engage in a true two-way dialogue. When employees come together in a team, they want their supervisors to be open to their ideas and suggestions, listening and giving them serious consideration and, most important, involving them in the decision-making. And when they do well, they want informal kudos as well as official recognition – praise for a job well done. They expect their managers to pay attention to what they do and to acknowledge when they achieve above-and-beyond results.

As you examine companies that kept employees during the boom days, they seem to have one thing in common: an awareness that the kind of job satisfaction that is behind employee retention isn't one single program, but a culture that recognizes the worth of its employees, trains supervisors to coach and nurture their employees, and reports employees with challenging assignments and $$$s for a job well done.

Frequently Asked Questions (FAQs)

Q1: What are the benefits of being an "employer of choice" – that is, a company that talented people want to work for – in good and bad economic times?

A: See Chapter 1.

Q2: What are some new techniques to recruit employees for hard-to-fill positions?

A: See Chapter 2.

Q3: What is behind the loss of employee loyalty – and subsequent high attrition?

A: See Chapter 3.

Q4: How can your company's Website support recruitment of IT personnel?

A: See Chapter 4.

Q5: How has technology facilitated recruitment of nationals from other countries?

A: See Chapter 5.

Q6: What makes employees leave?

A: See Chapter 6.

Q7: In tough times, how are leading companies reversing the "us vs. them" mentality to ensure more mobile, talented employees remain?

A: See Chapter 7.

Q8: What do managers and employees expect of their employers?

A: See Chapter 7.

Q9: Which online recruitment sites should you check out?

A: See Chapter 9.

Q10: How can you ensure you hire high performers?

A: See Chapter 10.

Index

Printed and bound by CPI Group (UK) Ltd, Croydon, CR0 4YY

13/04/2025

14656561-0005